S0-ADE-575

FOR MEN ONLY:

"**HOW TO MAKE YOUR WIFE YOUR MISTRESS**
is written for men—although more than a few will leave
it in an obvious place hoping their wives will read it out
of curiosity. And most of them should, for even better
reasons . . . The book's message is clear, concise and
valid: If you want a lover, then build a lover!"

—Marriage

FOR WOMEN ONLY:

HOW TO MAKE YOUR WIFE YOUR MISTRESS
is the most rewarding how-to book you'll ever give your
husband. It's a how-to about you! A daring, intimate,
no-holds-barred, woman-to-man talk about exactly how a
man should make physical love to his woman. "The author
tells it straight, . . . [without] coyness or cuteness . . .
A wise, witty, blithe-hearted book designed to add zest
to tired marriages!"

—Seattle Times

FOR LOVERS ONLY:
HOW TO MAKE YOUR WIFE YOUR MISTRESS

How to Make Your Wife
Your Mistress

—LOIS BIRD

HOW TO MAKE YOUR WIFE YOUR MISTRESS

*A Bantam Book / published by arrangement with
Doubleday & Company, Inc.*

PRINTING HISTORY

*Doubleday edition published August 1972
2nd printing ... September 1972
3rd printing ... September 1972
Bantam edition published January 1974*

To
JOSEPH,
the perfect lover

Contents

What She
Hasn't Told You
About Women—and Isn't
Likely to

There has probably always existed a credibility gap between men and women. Do you think Antony really swallowed the line Cleopatra fed him? Did Juliet believe Romeo was sincere in seeking a "meaningful relationship" or just another guy on the make underneath her balcony? To every man and woman who say, "I want us to be completely open and honest with each other," I have to ask, "Are you kidding?" Boy-girl games are liberally laced with lovely deceits. Take them away, and half the fun of the games goes with them. I want a man who will tell me lies, and a man who will pretend to believe the lies I tell him. Without those delicious lies of loving, seduction ceases. It turns

into rape or a bartered agreement. And seducing and
being seduced, as far as this gal is concerned, are two
of life's greater pleasures, my favorite indoor and out-
door sports. (If it isn't yours, stop reading here and go
back to your night baseball. I like baseball too, but
let's face it!)

The lies, however, can be carried too far, and in the
wrong direction. And they have been, mostly by us
females. We have, my male friend, conned you, and
conned you well. You have been *had*—a thought
which may have occurred to you once or twice. Your
mother probably started the deception. She was a
woman, and from her you learned what women are
really like—only they aren't! I'm not going to jump
on Philip Wylie's bandwagon and use Mom's head for
a base drum, but in the name of *honesty* (and for
once, that's the name of the game), we shouldn't let
mother off the hook. She served you a heaping platter
of womanhood all garnished with apron strings, flannel nightgowns, and peanut butter sandwiches. I'll bet
you never thought of dear old Mom enjoying a wild
romp in the hay or reading a good dirty book in the
afternoon while you were in school. Mom had an image as carefully cultivated as Richard Nixon's. There
were, and are, good mothers (98.4 per cent) and a
very few bad mothers (1.6 per cent). Good mothers
were devoted to their kiddies, loved puttering around
kitchens and flower gardens, making sacrifices, culti-
vating hobbies like needlepoint, PTA, and sainthood,
and, in general, being as exciting and excitable as a
pregnant tortoise. Bad mothers were devoted to all
sorts of "bad" things: They were turned on by men
(and horror of horrors, they showed it!), they drank
martinis, and they thought climbing up on a cross of
housewifery was a dumb way to spend an otherwise

pleasant afternoon. They might have enjoyed their kids, but they didn't turn down a weekend shackup with the children's father.

Good mothers never climbed in the sack except to sleep. Once in a while, they would submit to "conjugal relations" as their "wifely duty" (a conclusion drawn from our own existence: She must have done it at least once or we wouldn't be here, although she might prefer we accept virgin birth). Good mothers placed a lot of stock in anniversary gifts, proper table manners, considerate husbands, obligations to parents, correct impressions, paying bills on time, toilet training, church attendance, Mother's Day, and a balanced diet. The question "Sex?" was to be answered *Male* or *Female*, never "Yes, I sure do, and I like it!"

Thus the first image: *Woman, the marble statue.* Sensual? Never. Fun-loving? Seldom, and then only with her children. Sexy? Are you serious?

Every girl is raised to be frigid. And yes, I did say every girl. Even without a mother who gave her the marble statue image, she was taught an "I can take sex or leave it alone" female role. Oh, not that she believed the role. Unless she was thoroughly brainwashed to the point of turning off her head and hormones, she knew what she felt, and her biology was still her biology—and it was a sexy one. But admit to it? Never! At least not to a man. What would he ever think of her?

Deception? You better believe it! Remember what used to go on on those teen-age dates. You'd take her to a dance, and with the lights down low, you would pull her in close and she would press her pert little breasts against what you hoped she thought was your manly chest. You caught a whiff of that drop of perfume she had carefully applied to her cleavage and it turned you

on, didn't it? Then it sometimes got a bit awkward.
You didn't dare let her feel that bulge in your trousers.
She would be horrified. She might scream, faint, or
break out in hives. Who knows? So you bent at the
waist while still trying to dance cheek-to-cheek and
she never knew; she just danced on with that adoring
look in her eyes. What if she had told you the truth,
that you hadn't managed to keep your masculinity that
well hidden and that she enjoyed knowing she could
arouse you, that she even found it excited her? There
would go the image, bits and pieces of marble shattered all over the dance floor! So she played the *lit-
tle-wide-eyed-girl-who-hasn't-learned-about-the-birds-
and-bees* role to the hilt. Your mother, to say nothing
of her mother, would have been pleased.

Then on the way home from the dance, the game
really got cute. You drove out to that inspiration point
and parked. She didn't say, "Hey, where are you
going; that isn't the way to my house." She rode along,
chattering about who was at the dance with whom and
what she thought of Mr. What's-his-name, her history
teacher. She never would have dreamed what you had
on *your* mind. Well would you believe it was the same
thing she had racing through her pretty little innocent
head?

She'd sit there gazing up at the moon while you put
your plan into operation: the right arm around the
back of the seat, the distracting small talk, the long
drawn-out kiss while you fumbled around with impossible snaps, buttons, and zippers, and then, with one of
your hands down as far as possible and the other up as
far as she would allow, would come the lilting question
of naïveté: "What are you doing?" She even managed
to ask it with a straight face, wide eyes and all. She
knew very well what you were doing, every step of the

way. She knew what you were going to try to do before you ever left the dance, in fact, from the time you asked her for the date. If you hadn't played out the whole scenario step-by-step, she might have wondered if she had forgotten to read the deodorant ads. And why did she go along with it? Because she wanted to thank you for a great evening? Because she knew every boy expects it? Because she wanted to entice you into going steady? Forget it. Her reasons were pretty much the same as yours: She was turned on, and what you were doing gave her all sorts of nice, raunchy feelings. You may have wanted to score a conquest or prove your masculinity. She just wanted to feel good, and what you did to her made her feel very good indeed. Emotionally as well as physically.

And this brings me to the first of the well-kept secrets: *A woman thinks more about sex, wants more sex, and gets more from sex than a man.* Sorry. But that's the way it is. I know all about that virility bit and the much sought masculine stud image, and the fact that men want to believe they can arouse feelings she never would have had if it hadn't been for her tiger of a prince charming. I feel like kind of a heel bursting the bubble, but I promised to be candid and reveal the very naked truth. Sexually, women have it all over men. I've never been a man, but I don't have to be to know that much. Count the areas of that male body of yours that can feel erotic, those places she can touch and caress to really turn you on and send you up a tree. I don't mean where does it feel good to be touched. You could answer, "All over." I mean really GOOD good, what the sex manuals like to call "primary erogenous zones" (which always sounds to me like an area on a military map). How many do you find? Right! That's the same number I get. One! Oh, of course there may be a few other spots she can do nice things to, but for the most part, your sexual anatomy as a male is pretty well limited to you know where.

Us gals? Now there's a different matter, and I'm sure you already see what I mean. Just about every square inch of our surface, head to toe, can be triggered when you touch it in the right way. A hand to the inside of our thighs, a caress to the small of the back, a tongue run over our ear lobes, your lips brushing the back of our knees. They all turn us on. And I haven't even mentioned any "primary" spots.

But that's sensuality, not sex, I can hear some purist mutter. Well I have no desire to split hairs, but rubbing sun tan oil over my legs is a sensual experience. It feels nice, but that's about it. It isn't going to raise my pulse and passion unless I'm already in a very erotic state. But that same sun tan oil applied by his hands with just the right touch can make me forget all about sun-bathing, or even lying still that long. What man has "instant turn-on" skin like a woman?

And what about that glorious phenomenon we think and read about so much: *The Orgasm.* I know a number of gals who regularly reach climax more than once during love-making. More than once? Would you believe a dozen or more times? Sure, maybe not every time. Anyway, who's interested in keeping score at a time like that? But the point is, if a gal has shaken off all those anti-sex ideas she grew up with, she can certainly have the skyrockets go off more than once before the finale. How many men can do the same?

As for intensity, you've probably known women who screamed, moaned, cried, bit, scratched, and literally "went off" in a frenzy. You may be living with such a gal. Lucky you! Few men are ever so carried away. Conclusion: Women enjoy it more. Can anyone deny it?

In the interest of sexual equality and the abolition of that old double standard, I'm going to explode another female deception. Girls are taught to convince boys that in matters of sex females are incredibly stupid; they know from nothing! Don't you believe it. I'll bet when you were dating girls in high school you thought boys (and men) talked more about sex, compared experiences more, and knew more about what went on in the bushes and bed than your sisters and girl friends. We expected you to think that. We pretended to be so easily shocked. We acted appropriately "offended" if you talked of "nasty" things or dropped one of those four-letter words into the conversation. You found out masturbation could be fun and wouldn't make hair grow on the palms of your hands. Well, we discovered the same thing, maybe even sooner. And girls scribbled those same four-letter words on the walls of the girls' room you saw on the walls of the boys' room. I'll bet we even talked more about sex. Not in the same way, perhaps, but we did talk about it. Boys were more important to us than girls were to you, and we discussed boys to the point of tedium. We talked a lot of our own feelings toward guys. And we shared, usually with a best friend, what our boy friend wanted to do, tried to do, and did on our dates. Boys of the same age don't share much of their personal feelings. They boast and lie. They tell one another stories and jokes. But that's as far as it goes. Men sit in a barbershop reading *Playboy* and arguing the Giants chances for a pennant. You can sit in a beauty parlor and listen to women tell every last detail of what went on in bed the night before. And what they wish had gone on if their husbands hadn't been so inhibited and afraid of shocking them. It's all part of the game. We gals are supposed to be oh so sensitive—and dumb. The bedroom rule on roles says you are supposed to "introduce" us to the ways of sex, to guide us with much tenderness in the art of love, but always with the utmost concern for our feminine sensibilities. Boys are taught a girl may be shocked the first time she sees a penis. Mothers caution their sons to be very gentle with their brides on the honeymoon, the poor little girls will probably be scared half to death of that monster SEX. Some old family doctors even prescribe sedatives for the brides. She can then be a real sleeping beauty and miss all the fun!

Please! Don't treat us like we are scared little girls. We like sex. We like thinking about it, talking about it, dreaming about it. And doing it. We are not all puritanical little girls with hang-ups. Some of us may have some prudish rocks still bouncing around in our heads, but you don't help us shake them loose by treating us like cloistered nuns. Any healthy grown-up gal would much rather hear her man say, "Honey, I'd love to lay you" than "Darling, will you have marital relations with me tonight?" And all those other varieties of love you've heard about and thought about. We've heard about them too, and we also have fantasies. Lead on!

What about all those sex books, pictures, and movies? Again, we have been put in a box—an anti-sex stereotype. Somebody said we weren't supposed to be turned on by such things and the men believed it. Some of us even believed it ourselves (and then felt guilty and a little abnormal when a sexy passage in a book gave us those delightful "improper" feelings). If we played the expected phony role, we acted outraged when we caught you reading one of those "disgusting" magazines or when you suggested going to a "dirty" movie. ("My mother warned me what men were like!")

Sure, the books and movies aren't produced for us. They're designed to turn on men, which is sort of unfair, but so long as you don't believe we enjoy them and we won't admit we do, that probably won't change. If we can accept our own sexuality, however, we can be turned on by the same books and movies. You see more of the female anatomy in those movies than you do of males, and many of them throw in a lesbian act or two, but that doesn't turn us off so long as it isn't too kinky, boring, or just plain ugly. It doesn't mean we are all a bunch of female homosexuals. It means only that objects, pictures, and stories related to sex are sexually stimulating. Period. Sexual arousal is fun. Why shouldn't we like it as much as you do? I just wish they could balance those books and movies for us gals—and perhaps throw in just a little bit of plot. Why do you see so few of us at the porny movies? When was the last time you asked us?

You have fantasies, don't you? You know, those wild thoughts of sexual acts, erotic settings, exciting partners, and the rest. Well, so does that gal you're sleeping with. She isn't apt to tell you. We don't admit such things to men. But if I were to make a bet, I'd wager that women have more and richer fantasies than men. Even if you cross-examine us or give us the third degree with the overhead light shining in our eyes (all the time begging for a cigarette), we still won't admit the sexy daydreams we have had.

O.K., I'll tell the truth. I'm not, of course, saying this is true of me, but I do know it fits most women—whether they admit it or not. Just about every woman can remember her teens, lying in her bedroom masturbating and fantasying being raped, being seduced, being taken by a nameless, faceless man. She can recall the times she developed mythical relationships with a fantasy lover who spent languorous hours doing things to her which felt oh so good. She may have gone beyond her hands. She may have experimented with the handle of her hairbrush or whatever sparked her imagination. She grew up and her fantasies became less faceless. They were attached to the boys she dated. From the time she found herself turned on by you, her fantasies turned to you. You never knew it, but she spent more than a few pleasant hours in sexy daydreams of probably very improbable things you might do with her, to her, and for her. They were improbable because you never in this wide world would have guessed she would have had such far-out thoughts, and if you had tried out some of them, she would have felt compelled to play the shocked little virgin game (even ten years out of high school and twelve years out of the virgins' club).

Unless for some reason you have a thing for women's magazines, you probably are unaware how much the fiction we read feeds our erotic fantasies. Somebody once called it "pious pornography," a pretty apt description—if pious is another word for dishonest. You see, we cover up our pornography: we dress it in layers of crinoline and moonbeams. If a man wrote a 1972 version of *Gone with the Wind*, the reader would learn more details of Scarlett O'Hara's sexual anatomy and what she did with it with whom than her psychoanalyst or her gynecologist. But the author of that tale of a Southern belle seductress was a woman who knew her own sex. She knew women didn't need all those acrobatic descriptions and anatomical dimensions. We have imaginations more explicit than any of those San Francisco skin flicks. Give us a romantic plot and a couple of believable characters and you can do a fade-out at the bedroom door. Any gal can supply the rest from her own file of dreams and memories.

Here's something you may not know: Every woman would prefer to build her fantasies on memories of what she has shared with her man. But she can do so only if she has the memories to work with. That's where you come in. She isn't likely to be bored afternoons while taking that long bath and fussing with the pedicure and lotions and creams while she waits on your arrival if you've given her a filled back file of once-in-a-lifetime evenings, crazy exciting mornings, and lazy languorous afternoons; she'll have many memories to entertain her. That two hours on a deserted beach when you brought along the salami and wine and you both sunburned parts of you that had never been tanned can give her material for three volumes of fantasies. You may not remember the music that was playing on the car radio that night you parked up on that hill, but I'll bet she does. I'll wager my false eyelashes she even remembers the pattern of that motel wallpaper and the color of the shorts you were wearing. Do you? Of course not. Men are kind of "basic." We gals collect memories like a miser saving coins. The more the better. And the richer and more exotic they are, the more we can use them in our daydreams of dalliance. Give your gal the stuff on which dreams are built, and you'll keep her far better entertained than a TV rerun.

Want to know something else about us? We don't want to compete with men. Oh sure, I know all about those shrill hostile women's libbers who picket male bars and campaign for free abortions (for pregnancies

I think they hope would only happen through artificial insemination), but I also know they don't represent the average (spell that *normal*) male-loving gal. We know we can win the boy-girl game only when you win too. Nothing—but *nothing*—could be dumber than a battle of the sexes. No gal with her head screwed on right wants any part of such combat. You couldn't win with your mother. She held all the cards and she knew it and so did you. She could pin you in the corner and manipulate you out of your gold inlays. Talk about emasculation! Mother could not only snatch away your manhood, she could arrest its growth at a pre-adolescent level. Remember those times Mom would turn on the tears and you would feel totally "wiped out"? But that was Mom. And we don't want to play "mother" to our men. We know we can be "castrating females" anytime we choose. We don't want an emotional eunuch to share our bed and breakfast. We want a 100 per cent MAN. Seduce us and we'll submit. Cherish us and we will follow you. We want equality. We are not looking for a helpless little girl role. But we don't feel we have to prove our capabilities by running everything from the finances to the family car. We want to do our own thing and leave you alone to do your thing. We look to you to take over in those things which are yours, and we will handle our end of it. We like to be pampered. We enjoy being treated like a mistress, a much sought-after courtesan, the most desirable make in town. Give a gal half a chance and she'll deliver the loving care, concern, and cooperation that will make you the envy of every boy in the club.

Of course I can light my own cigarette. I can open the car door for myself, hold my own umbrella, and yes, even lay bricks if I take it into my head to do so, but playing female to a man's maleness is something every healthy woman enjoys. Regardless of what those "liberated" harpies say, we don't feel "put down" when you come on with some good old-fashioned chivalry. It tells us you recognize what we want you to recognize: that we are not "one of the boys"; we are women. We like it, and we're glad you like it. We want to keep those sex differences. If one of the "sisters" in the movement wants to seek "fulfillment" driving a bulldozer or carrying a picket sign, she's welcome to it. Every gal I know who is finding fun in living has found a man who is providing the biggest piece of it.

And there, lover, is one of those pesky paradoxes which may have made you wonder if you can ever understand women. A genuine, 100 per cent guaranteed woman needs a man and is willing to admit it. But she doesn't feel she must depend on a man or that he is necessary to her. A contradiction? Not really. In order to live my life to the fullest, I need sunlight, flowers, good books, laughter, the sound of rain, and the warm feel of a male body pressed against mine. Without them, I could probably go on existing, but I'm not sure it would be worth the bother. On the other hand, a mature woman is not a twelve-year-old or a mental midget. She is a very capable human being, a gal with a lot of moxie. She doesn't want or need a man to carry her through life. She wants a man to love, laugh, and live with. She doesn't need a security blanket.

We all know that helpless little girl role. We played it in high school. And *did* we play it! You must have wondered how we ever found our way in and out of the women's john. The word went around that guys are "threatened" by girls with brains. And even more turned off by a girl who can tell a carburetor from a bottle cap. Remember at those football games when we would scream at all the wrong times? We thought you'd like us better if we acted like dumb-dumbs. Well we don't like the role and we don't think any but the most insecure male likes it any better. We don't want to be brainless mannequins or sex objects, but being your sex *objective* gives us some great pay-offs. We have brains and we can use them. If we couldn't, we would be just as boring in bed as at the breakfast table. We may pretend not to understand all those things you talk about: the complexities of your job, world economics, orbital flight, earned run averages, and the like, but it's just a carry-over from those days we played the sexy-but-dumb bit. Expect—no, demand —more of us and you may be surprised how much we can learn in a hurry. Every gal knows—or ought to know—that sexiness is not incompatible with brains and capability. In fact, it takes more than average brains to be truly sexy. If you've ever shacked up with a really dumb broad you know what I mean. We know you are a man. We don't have to try to prove it to you or ourselves by playing out this "big, bright, capable *you* and weak, dumb, inept little me" game. We know most of that "girl talk" is pretty stupid. Let us join you, and let us know you expect more from us than chatter about kids, cucumbers, and *I Love Lucy* and you will find that "alive" gal you want to take away for a weekend.

Which brings up the business of your male world vs. our female world. In a word, "Who needs it?" Those oh-so-married cocktail parties and neighborhood get-togethers with the women huddled in one room clucking about runny noses and hem lengths while the men sit in another room talking about sports, stocks, and politics, are throwbacks to the eighth grade dance with the boys on one side of the room and the girls on the other. It's enough to make any gal who likes men upchuck all over the canapés. We don't know how you feel about this "never the twain shall meet" social routine, but it doesn't do much for a normal man-loving girl. If we had wanted that kind of hen house life we would have joined a convent. It may not come as a startling piece of news to you, but we find most "girl talk" just about as exciting as a detergent commercial. Not that we dislike women. They're all right as far as they go. It's just that being red-blooded heterosexual gals, we like men even more. And if the women haven't broken out of that kiddies and kitchen box, their conversations have the appeal of a week-old salad. Ever wonder why so many women spend all that time on the phone talking with a "best girl friend" or running back and forth across the street having coffee with some pin-curl-headed fellow house frau. I'll tell you. Once she has grown up and learned how much fun men can be, she will take a man to talk with any day. If she is spending all that time with other gals, you can be sure it isn't by choice. It's because her man isn't filling a very important need. And she hasn't decided to have an affair—yet. If you want her to stay your gal and the kind of turned-on woman who makes you pass up a drink with the boys because you are in a hurry to get home to her, don't underestimate how strong her needs can be. Right at the top of the list is a need to have her womanhood affirmed by *her man*. You do this in a lot of ways, you know. In all the ways you act as her lover you tell her she is the woman you desire. And not just between the sheets. I'm sure you heard women who complain, "He only wants me for sex." Perhaps you wrote them off as frigid housewives who look on

a husband as somebody who brings home a paycheck
and repairs the plumbing when nagged. But just maybe a few of them have said it like it is. If you come
home and spread your backside in front of the TV
while she does the dishes, go bowling with a gang of
grown-up boy scouts while she sits with the kids, and
spend more time talking with your drinking buddy
across the back yard fence than you ever do with her,
she may darn well turn frustration into frigidity.

I know, and you know, that whether or not all the
world loves a lover, women sure do, and the world
can't help but offer a whale of a lot more to the really
great lover. And I'll tell you the most important secret
about women, one you may have already figured out
for yourself: Any man with a strong healthy interest in
the opposite sex can become a phenomenal lover. He
may be short or tall, skinny or fat, rich or poor. He
may have broad shoulders, flat feet, a Grecian nose,
thinning hair, or a deviated septum. No matter. He
can be a Don Juan, Romeo, Casanova, and Joe Na-
math all rolled in one. All it takes is an understanding
of what female buttons to push to get what kind of response. And that isn't really all so hard as most men
seem to think. Women are the greatest push-overs in
the world. We can be *had*, just as we can be made.
We'll even help along the way. Learn to manipulate
one of us and we will be all too happy—even eager—
to lie down and purr. The rest of this book tells you
some of the more tested ways to make that pussy cat
of yours purr to your heart's content.

CHAPTER TWO

What
Turns Her On

Now down to the business of what buttons to push to get the response from her you most want. Not the buttons on that body of hers. We'll get to that later. You first have to manipulate her into being willing and eager to be *your woman.*

Let me start by putting in a plug for manipulation. I think it's a lousy shame manipulation has been given a bad name by all those child experts and encounter group people. Someone once said the difference between rape and seduction was salesmanship, and manipulation is just a high order of salesmanship. Here you have already been spotted five points in the game before you begin. Not only do we gals want to be manipulated, we're eager enough at times to beg for it. We are willing to believe the most implausible lies if they are told us in the name of love. We may know we are being manipulated, but that doesn't spoil the game or the goodies we are getting one little bit.

I suppose every sixteen-year-old boy tries to develop a "line" he figures will score with the girls. And every one of you were sure the girls would be taken in by it and never tag it for the line it was. The same line was used on every gal, and may have helped you chalk up a few notches in your gun belt, proving how good a line it was, how gullible girls are, and what a teen-age Lothario you were. We wouldn't have told you then for anything in this world, but we are big boys and girls now, so I can confess something you may have guessed. We knew it was a line. After dating the first half dozen guys, we had heard them all. Teen-age boys have a lot going for them, but originality isn't their long suit. We knew most of those lines from memory. But you know something? We never tired of listening to them from guys we took an interest in. A line is a little bit like being whistled at if you're a girl. You know it probably doesn't mean anything, and the man doing the whistling may not mean anything to you, but it gives a gal some mighty nice feelings to know she rates a whistle. (Do your good deed for the week: Whistle at an obviously pregnant gal; it may make her forget those tired legs and aching back.)

We are still suckers for a line. We may have heard it ten thousand times, but those words still do nice things to us. There are lines, however, which have more turn-on value than others. Females are vain creatures and more than a little narcissistic. We like seeing something attractive when we look in the mirror. And *you* are our most important mirror. Every gal wants to believe she turns on her man, that he likes what he sees when she walks into the room, that he seldom fails to get nice lecherous thoughts when she steps from the shower. I'm sure she could be Marilyn Monroe, Sophia Loren, and Raquel Welch all rolled in one and she'd still never grow weary of hearing her man tell her what reactions she starts in him. And if she isn't a sex goddess, she likes it and needs it even more.

Those females who run around screeching about how they want to be valued for their mind not their body can't have too much of either one. Of course we are not just pumped-up rubber dollies, but we do have bodies and we like knowing the looks and touch of our body can get a rise out of you. Let her know she turns you on in special ways and what specific things about her arouse your interest. "You look nice tonight" is a compliment, and she isn't about to turn down any compliments, but it doesn't quite tell her she raised your blood pressure. When she wears that plunging neckline and leans over to have you light her cigarette, let her know what's going through your mind. Don't just tell her she has good-looking legs. Show her how much you enjoy running your eyes and fingers and, yes, your lips over them. We females all have hang-ups about some part or parts of our anatomy. A gal can stand before her mirror and see every imperfection, large and small, glaring back at her. She sees those freckles across her nose as if they were painted a luminescent purple, and she is sure you must see them the same way. That appendectomy scar she hides beneath her bikini looks a good eighteen inches long to her. If she has picked up a few stretch marks having babies, she is sure her tummy looks like a plowed field. Her legs are too short. Her thighs are too fat or too skinny. She's getting a little bulge at the waist and she's sure it looks like a tractor tire. And her breasts? They're always a disaster.

It starts about the time we enter our teens. Those miserable years when we seemed to be put together all wrong. We were fitted out in those ridiculous training bras but they didn't help either our bust line or our morale. Today, the budding adolescent girl goes bra-less, but she is no more self-assured when it comes to what she shows between her shoulders and waist. We know most men have a thing for breasts. We may tell you you're fixated on them, but that doesn't mean we don't like it that way. It's only that it does give us problems—and maybe a few tear-filled nights. We see you admire those centerfold nudes. We look at them too. Always an absolutely fabulous pair of youthful, large, but firm, breasts. Then we sit in front of our own mirror. Too small, too large, too saggy, or too something else. Never quite the way we would like them to be. Perhaps we gals are the ones fixated on the female bust.

Unless you married one of those models, chances are she knows she hasn't the perfect figure. She falls in with the rest of the 99.9 per cent of us. She tries to do the best (seduction-wise) with what she has. And given encouragement and self-confidence, what she can do with it is more than enough for even a demanding man. Maybe she is carrying a few pounds over the currently fashionable ideal. She knows it—painfully. Maybe she knows you like her slimmer. On the other hand, she might think you prefer a gal who is "pleasingly plump." Some men do, just as some guys go for small-breasted girls while others are turned on by a 48D. In any case, you don't help your own cause (getting that all-important response from her) by continually pointing out the "flaws" she is already very aware of. If she is small-busted, you don't help her ego by remarking on the typist with the "beautiful big knockers." Have some heart. Give us a chance to improve what we can improve. Don't rub salt in the wound reminding us of what we would like to change but can't or what we are already hard at work trying to change.

We know our men aren't running around with sweaty palms and aching loins lusting after our bodies twenty-four hours each day. We know all about those other things which fill your head, those other interests which compete with us. If you were really on the make all the time, sex might even get to be dull (a thought that's hard to imagine). But we do like the game. We enjoy the lies when you tell us with your words, eyes, and hands that you desire us. When you say, "Hey! I *like* that," when you walk into the bedroom to catch us brushing our hair in the nude, the passing caress when you take the cup of coffee we bring you, the shared fantasy of what you would like to do with us, give us those feelings of being women. And being *a woman to a man* is what pleasures a gal the most. If she has put on a few extra pounds, you can let her know you can be turned on by a trim waist and a cute bottom without making her feel like a slob. Every gal measures her "erection power," her ability to make men think of her in terms of overnights at a ski lodge and summer evenings of skinny dipping. The more confidence she has in her "erection power," the more she will work to increase it. Your words and actions supply that much needed confidence. Maybe you will have to tell some white lies. Is that so bad if it's what she wants to hear? Remember, she always knew you had a line, but she always greedily gobbled it up. She still will.

There is a further way you have of turning her on. It may not be as direct as an all-over massage with scented safflower oil, but it plays a big part in transforming her into your complete mistress. She needs to feel needed. You have the same need. We know that much. But her need to be needed can raise some problems. Unless she is supporting you or has taken over running your life from your mother, she may have a hard time figuring out just what she gives you, what you really depend on her for. She pleasures you in bed, takes care of your things, keeps the place attractive to come home to, and sees to it you stay fed. But what else? Everything but sex would be routine for a housekeeper, and she knows that on your own you wouldn't have to look far for sex these days. You know that isn't all. If all you had wanted was a housekeeper and a bed partner, you wouldn't have married her. But does she know it? And please, don't just say, "She ought to know it." She needs to be convinced. And continually reassured that you rely on *her*. Rely on her for what? O.K., think about it for a minute. Isn't there really only *one* answer: You need her for *her*. Not for what she *does*, no matter how well she does it, but simply for what she *is:* your woman— lock, stock, and shackup, no holds barred, the gal who wants to pleasure you as you pleasure her.

Telling her you need her for herself, however, isn't likely to convince her. We live in a society which measures people on the basis of what they produce. And she is apt to evaluate herself using the same criteria, with the result that she sees herself in terms of dishwashing, floor scrubbing, and all those other "busy" chores. And believe me, it isn't much, and not near enough to make her feel you find her all important to your life. For its turn-on value, try letting her know how much she gives to you with her encouragement. Tell her what her satisfaction means to you. Let her know what her support does to give you the incentive to go on. You need to know she believes in you and will follow you because she has faith in you. She needs to know you recognize this need and rely on her faith. If you don't tell her, she'll never know. And she needs to know. It turns her on.

I'll tell you something else that keeps her hormones active and functioning in your direction: *talk*. I don't like to generalize, especially about my own sex, but I think I must say most of us gals like to converse with our men. And many if not most of you guys are the "strong, silent" types. It's part of that virile image, isn't it? We can understand it, but that doesn't pacify us. We still have that gut-level desire to share our thoughts and desires with you and have you share with us. Every gal has a need to know that her thoughts and opinions have some value to her man. What do you talk about? Everything and anything. So long as you let her know you are interested in what she has to say, that's all that is important. You're not asking her to take over and run things just because you seek her advice. It doesn't even mean you have to follow her advice. Just knowing you value what she may think is enough to turn her on. If she isn't working outside the home, she probably doesn't have too much opportunity during the day for any intelligent adult conversation. Slim chance the gal next door is going to come up with anything apt to stimulate her brain cells. She gets hungry for grown-up conversation with her man. It helps keep her alive. And most important, it reassures her she is important to you—which is the biggest turn on of all.

Every gal is addicted to two things, and one of them, in case you haven't guessed, is romance. This whole book, plus several more, could be written about romance and what it means to us. I suppose in a way it is. You see, when it comes to being turned on, romance is the key that fits every gal's lock. Take romance out of it, and you might just as well keep your boy-girl games. Woman does not live by hormones alone!

Not that men don't dig romance. We know you do. But we also know something else: Romance is not something which is taught to boys as it is to girls. We developed a mighty strong appetite for it about the time we tried out our first lipstick. That's what made up the biggest part of those fantasies—at least until they became more "basic." We became incurable romantics with no interest in a cure. We know, on the other hand, the picture you and every other man was given of romance. It wasn't quite manly. Right? "To hell with the moonlight and gardenias; let's just have a roll in the hay." Wasn't that more the he-man approach? If you wrote any love notes, you can be sure she kept them. But I'll bet you would have rather lost your left foot than have your buddies read them. Romance is one more department in which males get consistently short-changed.

It is also something women talk about but never define. She says, "I want him to be a romantic lover." Fine. But ask her to describe a "romantic lover." She may give a few examples of what the romantic lover of her dreams might do, but that doesn't help much. If she says a romantic lover brings her flowers, any guy knows that flowers, even twice a day, are not enough to give him the image of a romantic lover. In about three days, he'd be broke and he'd feel like a florist's delivery boy.

Since most women want romance, never get too much of it, find it the basic ingredient to any ultimate turn-on, but don't want to explain what it is they want,

I'll try to describe the essentials of what we gals mean when we talk of things "romantic."

To begin with, romantic actions, places, and things always have some element of the unexpected. A single long-stemmed rose you bring her when there is no special occasion is romantic. If you brought a rose every Tuesday and Thursday month after month, the romance value would be lost. And I'm afraid this is where an awful lot of men fall down. They become creatures of habit, and when routine creeps in, romance fades away. I'm sure this isn't you, lover, but how many guys do you know who stick to that husband-type dating? You know: Dinner (always at the same restaurant) and a movie, or Dinner *or* a movie. She may like the food at that place. She might even be a nut for the cinema. But in time, the repetition will chip away the romance.

I'm sure it isn't easy to come up with bright new ideas. And if you live in River Bottom Corners, population 118, the Hiway Diner and the Vogue Theater may be just about all there is. Romance can be injected, however, into just about anything you do together. Let's start with this matter of "dates." I know the idea of dating is supposed to be kind of passé. It's corny and square, something out of another age—or another age group. Who needs all that Emily Post "the gentleman invites the lady to accompany him to the ball" jazz? We did that back in those pre-married, *bring-the-girl-a-white-orchid-for-her-wrist* days. We outgrew all that, didn't we? Well, didn't we? Not if you're female. The whole bit may be as hokey as a Rodgers and Hammerstein musical, but it massages a feminine ego spot that makes your kitten purr long and low.

Dating is not just "going out somewhere together."

It calls for certain do's and don't's. And much as I hate to give men a failing grade in anything, I'm afraid when it comes to dating, the average husband flunks out all the way. When was the last time you dated the gal who shares your bed? If she is your wife, and you're typical of your sex, I'll bet you didn't answer, "Last Saturday evening." Maybe you took her out, but was it a *date*? Don't sigh and throw up your hands. I know it must seem like females are simply never satisfied, that no matter what you try to give us, it isn't enough. I'll be the first to admit what every gal must deep down know: We're all just a little bit bitchy and demanding, and about half the time we don't know quite what we want ourselves. But it isn't really a date when you take us somewhere at the last minute because you are obviously bored with television. And it isn't a date when you ask, "Hey, you want to look in the paper and see if anything is playing at the movies tonight?" We want our men to plan the dates, to ask us out for the evening, and to *take* us. Something is missing when you rely on your gal to suggest where to go. And a big chunk of romance gets lost if she has to ask you to take her out. When you met and started pursuing her, you didn't wait for her to come up with all the ideas, did you? You psyched out what you thought would turn her on. And it worked. Why change it? She wants to feel she is someone very special to you, your woman, and that you want to *give* her the day or the evening. Those spontaneous times are great, but you know something? The ones that come off the best are not really so spontaneous after all. They may be "spontaneous" to her and look every bit like a "spur of the moment" surprise, but there has been some sharp thinking and planning on his part behind it or it wouldn't come off so well. I remember the times we've been walking by a Broadway theater just before show time and he has "spontaneously" suggested taking in a musical that has been sold out for weeks and has just happened to have a pair of tickets in his pocket. And again when he has "impulsively" taken me through the door of an exclusive little restaurant with a view of the ocean and a line of couples waiting for a table. And what do you know, he had reservations. That kind of "spontaneous" planning and pampering makes it the sort of romantic date that comes off without a hitch. And something else: I know he avoids feeling the letdown that comes from "flubbing" his male role when he does his pre-planning.

May I make another point about dating? And about romance? Maybe it has something to do with our female vanity and some of those lingering feelings of insecurity, but we want you to date us because you want to be with your woman. A *date* means one guy and one gal, not a crowd. That double-dating routine is all right for the junior prom and for garden club matrons, but not for a *man* and a *woman* with the right chemistry going for them. Take a look at those couples who "double." Talk about pathetic! The two house fraus end up talking together, and their men end up doing the same. Exciting? A little less than a game of solitaire. If you have fallen into that suburban double-date thing, who is responsible? If you are the one who suggests dragging along another couple (and you can be sure they don't have much of a great affair going for them or they wouldn't accept the invitation), stop and think what this communicates to that gal of yours. Is she going to be convinced you want to be with her? Or is she going to feel you find her boring and that you would rather have one of your cronies along to talk with? Whatever she may think, she isn't likely to get the idea you have romance in mind—unless you have a pretty kinky notion of romance. What happens if you want to stop out in the woods on the way home to try one another's charms by moonlight? Do you suggest to the other couple that they listen to the car radio while you take a short hike into the bushes? Are you going to go on talking politics with that clown sitting in the back seat while your gal sneaks down your zipper? Not unless you have one of those things for "groups." If you do, all I can say is, "Do your own thing but count me out; one real *man* can supply all this gal desires, and I won't give him any reason to seek more than I can provide." If she is the one who always seems to want to include someone else when you take her out, is it because you usually spend more time ignoring her than showing her you want to be with her? Or is she just keeping up her membership as one of the girls in the flannel nightgown set? If it's the latter, maybe it is time you put down that masculine brogan of yours and let her know you are interested in dating *her*, not the other members of the sorority. If you don't, you may wake up some morning to find yourself missing a pair of gonads.

One thing needs to be said and underscored about this business of dating. Most guys have a hang-up about the finances of dating. They feel a date has to be something that runs the budget into three columns of red ink in order to qualify. It doesn't. There probably isn't one gal in a thousand who judges a date on the basis of how much the guy spends. If you have a female who gets her kicks for the evening out of seeing you spend the whole bankroll and then some, she belongs working in Fort Knox. Send her off to Washington and find yourself a genuine woman. It may take a little more thought and imagination to come up with a date when your wallet is on the thin side, but imagination is one of the biggest elements in creating romance. If you lived in New York City, you could take her to dinner at The Four Seasons and follow it with orchestra seats for a musical at the Palace. You could part with over a hundred dollars without half trying. Or, you could pick up a pair of pastrami sandwiches to go and watch the lights of the city from the deck of the Staten Island Ferry. Which rates highest in romance value? Ask her.

A date could be a window-shopping stroll after the stores have closed. It could be a free orchestra concert at the local junior college. It might be riverbank fishing by moonlight without too much attention to the fishing. Those big evenings out with the waiter scooping the sour cream and chives into the baked potato and the bottle of red wine you ask him to open "to let it breathe" are great and we love that kind of "specialness." But those "shoestring" dates offer a high level of romance. They say to a girl: "What we do together is not all important; it's just being with you that makes it a time to remember."

To return to our big broad question of what makes romance (defined, of course, from the female perspective): Romance is, in a way, the unnecessary gesture. And there! That ought to explode your cortex after I just got through making the heavy point of how necessary it is to a gal's distaff ego. It is important. Romance is what keeps her eagerly bedded rather than bored. It is the romantic *action* which is "impractical." Take an example: Walking in the rain doesn't make much in the way of good sense, does it? If it was sprinkling when you left your office on a Friday afternoon and you decided to walk around the city in that sogginess for an hour before going home, you'd probably have a few loose seeds in your gourd, right? But walking with her in the rain, and pressing your wet lips together underneath a chestnut tree while the passing cars made the sounds of frying bacon on the pavement and the water trickled down the back of your necks and she let her hair-do dissolve into matted strings, that's *romantic*. Being more than a little bit crazy, it's more than a little bit romantic.

Eight hours sleep and a balanced diet are good and sensible (mother would nod her approval). A night on the beach with cheese and a bottle of red wine isn't what the doctor ordered, unless the doctor believed *living* was more than what the insurance companies talk about. Romance has rules of its own, and the rules will never make sense to the purists and the puritans. They're an unromantic lot. They've never had a good you-know-what in their lives. A sensible husband would never take his wife into the shower in her negligee and rip it off her, would he? Of course not! It would be not only impractical and wasteful, it would be rather lustful, even animalistic. You bet! And romantic! And horny! And packed full of delicious liquescent (like that word?) feelings!

I remember talking with a gal who complained her husband never gave her any "personal" gifts; it was always something for the house. She let him know about it, and for Christmas he gave her a flannel nightgown "with blue bunny rabbits on it." In the romance department, he strikes out without ever swinging. Of course fairness compels me to say she is about as sexy as a carton of cabbage, but he sure doesn't light any fuses. It might be fun to see what a guy with a high combination of glands and glamor could do for that little mouse.

Romantic gifts are almost never the "sensible" ones.

She may need a new ironing board to the point of desperation, but as a gift, it rates a very low romance quotient. I'm not saying don't give her the ironing board. But don't make all your gifts those practical items you know she needs. Why not a wine carafe for the bedroom? Or something she can slip on in the evening, sheer enough to read your newspaper through? A recording of that song you listened to together on your last weekend away? A volume of love poems? Two matched cups for the morning coffee you share? A "telephone shower" attachment for her bath?

Any gift says, "I love you," since love is a "gift of self." The romantic gift says, "I've *fallen* in love with *you*." A romantic gift is not the sort of thing you give to your maiden aunt—let's hope. And the same can be said of romantic words and gestures. They all convey, "I want to have a love affair with you."

Know what else turns a woman on? Having a "forbidden fruit" love affair. You may have thought only men feel the clandestine affair offers an added bonus of stimulation. We gals are supposed to be locked-in on hearth, home, and security. And we may like sex but we think without benefit of a wedding band, the whole business is tawdry. Well don't you believe it. Becoming something of a scarlet woman is part of a healthy gal's fantasies. Naughtiness has a particularly feminine appeal. I'm not saying she has designs on the guy who reads the gas meter. If she has a lover who keeps her well satisfied, why would she? But that doesn't mean the role of mistress isn't more appealing to her than that of wife. Maybe you've put a ring on her finger, but that doesn't have to mean the end of the affair. I heard of a gal who worked out a clever game with her husband. Every so often she would phone him at his office during the day to say, "My

husband is away; are you free this afternoon?" The
two of them would make plans to meet at an out-of-
the-way motel. They would each drive their own car
and he would be waiting when she got there. Afterward, they would leave separately. She would go back
home and he would return to his office. That evening,
neither one of them would in any way talk about how
they had spent the afternoon. The affair stayed a secret between two lovers. Such an elaborate game may
strike some *marry-and-settle-down* types as utterly ridiculous. Believe me, it carries great pay-offs. Not
only is it a great preventative medicine to combat
boredom, it provides the excitement of wantonness,
which serves to increase the tempo of her pulse and
passion.

I've talked to a lot of gals who don't find sex with
their husbands much more exciting than gin rummy.
No more satisfying than a foot massage. Pleasant, perhaps, but . . .

This is the girl who, before she exchanged those
vows, would develop damp thighs and glazed eyes just
sitting beside her man at a bus stop. She took an over-
heated motor on her honeymoon and she stayed
revved up all through the first year or two. Then gradually some of the spark plugs misfired and she found
her motor harder to get started. If sex, for her, didn't
die, it at least didn't remain wide awake. Of course,
she doesn't want it that way. Who would? She would
like nothing better than to return to those lusty days
when she was learning how he takes his coffee and
discovering what side of his face he shaves first. She
may know what has happened but sees no way to
overcome it. She suffers from a creeping malaise
called the marriage doldrums (for want of a better diagnosis). Like summer colds, every gal is liable to

catch a touch of it from time to time. Her man isn't responsible for it; he didn't give her the germs. But he can provide the cure. Later on, I'll be talking about this whole social box we call marriage and the meanings our laced-up society has given it. That's where the collapse of the romance begins. Try to remember how you learned about the joys of S-E-X. Husbands and wives did it to make babies, but only the unmarried (to each other) did it for *fun!* Those doldrums and drab sex come when she discovers that, what do you know, she really *is* married. No longer any fears of getting caught. It's now all legal—with license to prove it. Seduction? Why bother? The license did away with all that.

A man with an enviable record with women once summed up his secret of successful seduction as follows: "If she's a whore, treat her like a queen. If she's a queen, treat her like a whore." (Right on! Male Chauvinist of the Year!) I'm not sure just how he meant it or how far he carried his policy, but I'm willing to give my interpretation: The boy-girl sex game has a way of becoming a big fat bore if it isn't varied. Unless she's tied in knots of insecurity and rigidity, a gal quickly tires of playing the same role with her man day after day. Just as she enjoys change and imagination when it comes to dating activities, she craves the pleasantly unexpected when it comes to sex roles. If she stops to think of it, every woman knows that the majority of men are creatures of habit, and more so than the female of the species. It isn't all a sex difference. Most of you have lives which are regulated and regimented into a nine-to-five box. You even have bosses who like office procedures, décor, and dress about as casual and creative as a Marine barracks. And maybe this has something to do with why men find it so difficult to vary their roles when it comes to romancing women. Men have a way of becoming totally married and settled down quicker than women. She may fall into that gray little box of housewifery with soap operas and Early American kitsch bedrooms, but it isn't what the gal who longs for living with a capital "L" dreams of. She doesn't want a *husband;* she wants a *lover.* In fact she wants several lovers, but she wants them all wrapped up in the same man. She's adaptable, and she likes adapting. (If she doesn't, she is missing a lot out of life; she hasn't much to give to a man; she has problems; and she should run to her nearest shrink.) There may be times when she digs the rough crude approach à la Stanley in *Streetcar Named Desire:* "I'm going to tear your clothes off and give it to you here on the floor." Not in actual hostility, of course, but in a way that communicates pure, out-and-out lust for her. There are other times she is fully turned on by the Continental lover approach: violets, love poems, and kissed fingertips— the sound of violins, and the lights on the Grand Canal of Venice. And there are even times when she enjoys playing lover-slave to her man: taking over the aggressive role and serving his desires, whatever they may be. I could mention a dozen more, but you get the idea. If her man lays the right kind of groundwork (and that's mostly a matter of lavishing her with love and showing her, at all times, how much she turns him on), he will find his woman more than eager to follow his lead. But she wants him to *take* the lead. She doesn't want to be the one to introduce the romantic games. Sure, she could come up with the suggestions, and she doesn't mind in the least playing the aggressor (unless she's sitting on an emotional cake of ice), but even where she seduces him, she wants to feel that this is in some way his choice: that he is seducing her into seducing him. And that he sets the mood and the roles for the occasion, keeping her eager and off guard.

In capsule form, the rule for turning on any red-blooded gal from sixteen to sixty is: *Never become her husband; stay her lover.* Love and romance are for youth, and age is more in your head than the rest of your body. She doesn't want a tired old man who treats her to a *good-old-reliable-mother-to-my-children* "affection." The one who said, "The only difference between a rut and a grave is the depth of it," spoke a real truth. If you have fallen into that nine-to-five, sex only after the late news, camping vacations always with the kids along, six-pack-of-beer mentality *rut,* you're dead and you don't know it. And just as if it's news to anyone: No gal likes making-out with a corpse. If you fall into that no-imagination, take-her-for-granted cadre of ho-hum husbands, don't be shocked when you come home to find the milkman delivering more than four quarts of homogenized and a pint of whipping cream. Remember, I warned you.

CHAPTER THREE

What
Turns Her Off

In Mario Puzo's novel *The Godfather*, the old mafia leader questions his underlings about the strength of an opponent by asking, "Has he got balls?" He could have asked the same question by listing off the attributes of strength, courage, ability, perseverance, self-reliance, and maybe a few more. "Has he got balls?" is shorter and says it all, and a lot more.

It also puts into words what a woman asks herself when sizing up a man. When they were little girls, big girls grew up on tales of beautiful princesses who were snatched from the lairs of dragons and rescued from the clutches of villains by the strong, brave, and handsome prince. It didn't matter that the poor dope took chances in doing so that marked him an idiot with a death wish; they weren't even queasy at the thought that he was formerly a frog. If he proved he had "balls," that was enough. Little girls have a way of becoming big girls without ever losing their dreams of the rescuing prince. But worse luck, a good prince is hard to come by these days, even second hand. All the good ones seem to be already claimed by some not-so-slumbering princesses. A gal may settle for the court jester or the foppish little dauphin, but she'll only give the key to her inner chamber to a genuine card-carrying Prince Charming. Even those old fairy tales were loaded with all sorts of juicy Freudian stuff. (Just read some of those psychoanalytic journals about the unconscious meaning of the prince penetrating the thicket to awaken the sleeping beauty—talk about racy stories!)

Fortunately for would-be lovers, you don't have to be born to this royalty. The manhood she's looking for in a mate is more guts than genes. You were born male, but you had to learn to be a man. We know it doesn't come easy, and we wouldn't trade places with you, but we know we need you to be a man if we are to respond with our womanhood in all the ways you want it. If all the gals who complain, "He isn't a *man*," were lined up, they'd comprise quite an army of frustrated females. And you know something? I don't think most of their men are really aware what it is that gripes them so much. All they know is that something turns her off.

Let me try to clear up the mystery. A woman wants to be able to give herself to her man, to surrender willingly to him and follow his lead. (Obviously, I'm talking about a *real* woman, not the counterfeit women who want to prove they can take any male to the mat two falls out of three—and refuse to give in and have some fun when they do get down on the mat.) But in order to swing along with him wherever he leads, she has to be able to trust him. When that confidence crumbles, she pulls back. And when she pulls back, you're liable to find yourself in a bed that's about as warm as a winter day in the Arctic.

What undermines that confidence? It could be several things. Complaining, for example. O.K., so life isn't all cold gin and caviar, but wringing your hands and whining to her about what that abrasive world is doing to you isn't going to change much of anything —except maybe the way she sees you. Maybe your boss *is* the sort who pulls wings off flies and seems to have the fly paper out for you. Can she really bail you out of it? Do you want her to go down and poison the coffee in the executive lunch room? Or find a job to support you so you can thumb your nose at the old man and walk out? If you are not looking for her to rescue you, don't lay the complaints on her. She'll begin to think you're looking for a mother, and let's hope that isn't what you want because you can be sure it isn't what *she* wants.

This goes as well for reciting a litany of other complaints. If you have a headache, hang-over, or hangnail, she may provide a shoulder to cry upon and a warm poultice of sympathy, but unless she's a faith healer, she probably can't do much more for you than you can do for yourself. Some gals, I'll admit, get their kicks out of playing nurse-mother to their men. They shove vitamins down them at breakfast, regulate their diets, remind them to have their yearly checkup, and, in general, fuss more than the trainer of a Kentucky Derby favorite. Unless he's so flaky he puts his trousers on over his head, no man needs that kind of "concern." And it's sure he isn't going to get much "swinging from a chandelier" fun with such a health nut. The gal who looks for a lover, however, doesn't want to stand around holding a crying towel for her mate. If you walk in the front door night after night with words and actions that say, "I'm tired, and beat, and wiped-out by the rat race," and wake up in the morning complaining of the gas on your stomach or the crick in your neck or the pain in your hemorrhoids, you're not doing anything for that virile image. I'm not saying you have to be the strong, silent type who smiles as he leads his troops into battle with both legs shot off, but if you are continually communicating a whining weakness to her, she cannot be expected to follow you with much confidence.

Probably the heaviest points on her scorecard of manhood will be given to *reliability* and *responsibility*. Fall short in those departments and her phallic fantasies won't stay turned to you for long. She wants to be a "kept woman" but she doesn't want to be kept hanging over a cliff. If the two of you were going sky-diving, would she trust you to pack her chute? Well if she is going to be your woman in all the ways that count, she has to jump just as far—and count on you to catch her. Break the news to her that you've taken a job washing elephants in Nairobi and what response do you want? Damn right! You want her to start shopping for pith helmets and mosquito netting with a smile. But unless you're sleeping with a gal who is apt to jump over Niagara Falls for a Saturday night bath, she isn't going to throw her reservations in the reservoir unless you have a proven track record of reliability and common-sense responsibility for her. Why should she? And this, my male friend, doesn't mean just that business of a pay check. You could have double the assets of Howard Hughes and still leave her in a state of chronic insecurity. She needs to be able to rely on *you*, not just a bank account. Look at it this way: Can she really believe you have her best interests

at heart, that she comes first before your golf game
and your mother? When you promise to be home for
dinner at six, can she be sure you won't stop off with
your buddies for a drink and show up, half-plowed, at
eight? Do you handle the business affairs of the family
with a modicum of good sense, or does she have to
wonder whether they're going to shut off the water because you forgot to pay the bill or blew the money on
a scuba diving rig?

She isn't an insecure little girl (at least I hope she
isn't for your sake as well as hers) and she isn't in-
competent. She is perfectly capable of running the
whole show herself. But when she has to take over and
see to it that the ship doesn't sink because her man fell
asleep at the tiller and ran them on the rocks, she begins to feel she has adopted a male child and lost a
man. And *that* feeling will cause any woman to turn
off.

A swing too far in the other direction can also flip
her switch to the off position. That patriarch bit with
the male lion seated at the head of the table playing
God went out with Teddy Roosevelt running his scout
troop up San Juan hill. We *have* come a long way,
baby. And so have you. You don't have to be super-
daddy to us, shielding us from the rocks and shoals of
life, handing down paternalistic dictums and advice.
You want an equal partner when you climb in bed,
don't you? The limp little girl who needs to have you
draw a diagram for everything isn't going to be much
of a frisky little filly. Having a man play the concerned
father to her is as dampening a prospect as being
asked to play mother to him. She has the brains to do
her own thing without a man telling her each move to
make. Being man of the house and lord of the manor
doesn't have to make you responsible for seeing to it

she keeps her teeth brushed and her grocery list within limits. And it sure as sin and taxes doesn't mean she must be talked down to. That Mickey Mouse machismo that makes some men treat women like they were the village idiots and couldn't be trusted to drive a car, balance a checkbook, or make a decision on anything more complex than which detergent will get their sheets whiter than the gal next door is enough to make a woman want to burn a jock strap or two—on the wearers! If you treat us like little girls all day, don't expect us to behave like big girls when you turn out the lights.

Want to know something else which turns off a woman? The guy who makes like a *clod*. And what do I mean by clod? I'm sure it isn't you, lover, or you wouldn't be reading this book, unless the gal who sits across from you at breakfast force-fed it to you. The clod is usually about as active as a toad filled with buckshot. He seldom shows much in the way of initiative, drive, or goals. And enthusiasm? About like a well-fed walrus.

The clods of this world are not losers. Nor winners. They are simply non-winners. The clod is content to lie down and allow life to roll over him. He seems to lack the juice flowing in his veins to go after much of anything vigorously, whether it be a job, a love affair, or some genuine fun. He became eighty years old within a year after he and his gal made it a twosome. He never appears excited about *anything*. At least not about anything which involves *her*. Oh, he may get excited enough to spill his beer when he's with his buddies at the baseball game, but when he walks through the front door at night or takes her out for a "big" evening (dinner, a movie, and home by eleven) he acts like he's recuperating from a two months' bout of malaria. Whatever get-up-and-go he may have once had got up and went. If her man isn't *alive*, she won't be—at least not for him. She wants a man who faces the world with ambition and enthusiasm as well as confidence, and with a certain *joie de vivre*. The knight on the white horse doesn't plod down the road like he is riding a tired mule, he charges into the battle of life, eager to win the prizes. And she is one of the prizes to be won.

She is also left flat by a man who takes her for granted. One of the great kicks in being a female comes from being pursued. And from knowing you are seen as pursuable. Nothing can be more of a turn-off, more of a letdown to the feminine ego, than to be treated like part of the home furnishings by the man in her life. One of the worst put-downs I've heard in a decade came from the mouth of a "happily married husband." Someone in the crowd brought up the topic of jealousy between spouses. "Have you ever been jealous where I'm concerned?" his gal asked him. "Never," he told her, "I can't even imagine you play-ing around with another guy; you're just not the type." If I had been in her panty hose I think I might have set out right then to prove just how far wrong he was. No gal wants her man to think she can be bedded by any male who rings her doorbell, but she sure doesn't want to be pegged as devoid of any glandular response or so blah she can't interest *any* men. If you went after her with passion and persistence before you made the whole thing legal, ask yourself: Have I given up the chase because I know she's my woman now? If you have, think again. She may still have your name and a ring on her finger, but she may have given up being *your woman* the second time you looked through her as if she wasn't there. And that works triple when it comes to sex. In those pre-married days you no doubt tried everything that came to your virile imagination to get her panting on a pillow. Seduction was your great obsession then, wasn't it? (If it wasn't, why wasn't it?) If you now act as if that marriage license did away with all that and as if a wife is supposed to provide a service in the way the heifer services the bull as part of her wifely "duty," you can be sure you will wind up sleeping with a gal who does it in just that way: as a duty. Every bit as active as a chunk of granite.

Some men act toward their gals about the way one might read a less than compelling book. Pick it up and browse through a page or two when in the mood, then leave it on the night stand for days or weeks and expect it to be there, untouched, when you get around to it next. You can see it at parties. The husband virtually drops his wife off as he enters the door and reclaims her only when it's time to leave. She could be three hours in a coma behind the couch and he'd never know it. But when they get home? You guessed it! She is supposed to melt at his first physical advance.

Which brings me to what is probably number one on the list of turn-offs, from what I listen to from other females: the way men approach sex.

If men were entirely responsible for the sexual satisfaction or lack of same of their women (and they are *not*), I might guess from what I hear women say that ninety-nine out of every hundred males are almost hopeless when it comes to love-making. They've learned what goes in where, but that is where the education stopped. A woman wants a *lover,* not a copulating robot.

As I mentioned a couple of chapters ago, we gals have a mighty complex sexual anatomy, and maybe an even more complex set of emotions. We know you, a man, can be ready, willing, and able as soon as you get an erection. That isn't to say you don't enjoy sex more when there are erotic games and variations and it isn't reduced to a quick three lunges and it's over. That quicky approach is for teen-agers in the back seats of cars and sailors in a border-town bordello. It's strictly nothing for lovers. And it scores zero with women.

But what is a gal to do? We are supposed to let the man take the lead, at least most of the time. Most gals like it that way, and we know the average male wants to be the aggressor. Not every time, of course. But he likes coming up with the ideas rather than having a woman who does the teaching and innovating. If her man always comes on with a basic "roll over and let's get to it" approach, she will quickly come to prefer the late show for her entertainment, and masturbation for her sexual drive.

She is turned on by a man who knows what he is doing when it comes to the art of love-making. And she is turned off by the guy who doesn't seem to have learned what it is all about. She doesn't necessarily want to know how you got your experience before you met her, but she appreciates the fact that you were not the bumbling virgin when you first took her to bed. She knows you had to learn somewhere and sometime, that you weren't born with a built-in knowledge of the *Kama Sutra* and the innovations of Casanova. If her own sex education and imagination have gone past the "this is how little babies are born" stage, she is well aware the whole business can—and should—go beyond the point of "doing what comes naturally." There are all kinds of things you can do to pleasure her. She wants a man who makes it a point to learn them. And practice them. Some, he may have read about. Which means he has taken the trouble (trouble?) to read books on sex. Others, he may have heard about and is willing to try, even if they may not *sound* like the greatest kicks. And some ideas may develop out of his imagination and trial and error experimentation. If he talks with her about sex in a free, mature, man-woman manner often enough (and if any of us stops to think about it, isn't sex a more fun topic than most of the things we hash over most of the time?), he may even learn that she can come up with some very creative suggestions.

I'm not going to try to cover all the things which might turn off a woman. In the first place, if you're living with her, you should be able to find out what turns her off if you make the effort to be observant. It may be that you scrape the skin off her when you don't bother to shave on weekends, or don't stop off in the shower on your trip to bed. Maybe it's the time you spend on the phone talking to your mother. Or the booze you always down before you take her to bed (to work up some false courage?). It may be that you never express your love for her (and just rolling her over on her back five minutes after you fall into bed following a night of bowling and boozing with the boys is *not*—repeat, *not*—an expression of love). If it's something that it makes sense to change, change it. And by that, I mean *IF* you discover you are doing something (or failing to do something) that has an effect on her which is less than what you desire, it makes sense (enlightened self-interest, lover) to change things.

But there is another reason I'm not going to go into some of the things which may turn her off: You might think I'm suggesting you go along with her desires when you shouldn't. Does that confuse you? Probably. All right, I'll try to explain. Let's say you find yourself with a gal who finds sex just about as appealing as a sack of wet mice, who is turned off by just about everything erotic, except maybe her own solitary sex-thing. Do you go along with it and "keep your distance"? Or what if she doesn't go for anything but the "missionary position" with the lights out, while you keep trying to talk her into some games with whipped cream on a water bed? Do you go along out of fear that to do otherwise would turn her off? Forget it! It won't get you what you're after. Never. Those dry old marriage manuals used to advise that sort of hands-off approach. ("While these acts are not in any way abnormal, the considerate husband will desist when he finds his wife is repulsed by any particular act.") And just where is that supposed to leave the guy with a hungup wife? Right! Just as hung-up. Just as frustrated. And just as bored by the whole sex scene. Giving in to her isn't the answer, and unless you have the same sex inhibitions, why would you want to? You can either let her know you expect a gal who is grown-up, sexwise, or you can find yourself a gal with her glands in gear and leave little frigid miss to that mental chastity belt of hers, or you can drag her off to an analyst's couch. Some things you can change. Some you can't.

Some advice from a gal who is biased in favor of men: Think over what I've said in the last two chapters. We all can get careless, and once in a while, we all need to take a look at ourselves. If you were a woman, you would always be aware of what turns on and turns off a woman. But you're not. So you have to learn—and keep tabs on—what will make it with that gal of yours. Score yourself on how you score with her.

That said and done, shall we get down to the art and science of serious seduction? That, after all, is where the winners leave the losers behind, and you *are* a winner, aren't you, lover?

CHAPTER FOUR

Seduction
and Other Games

You know what you want from her. Don't you? But I'll bet you can never bring yourself to let her know. It would leave that vulnerable male ego of yours hanging out in the breeze just waiting to be clipped. Every smart gal knows, however, and with the right kind of approach, she will deliver it up on a satin pillow.

Answer the following question: Do you want your woman to treat you like you are a combination god and genius? Did you answer, "No"? Then why not try answering the question again, only this time tell the *truth*. Of course you want her to think you can walk on water. What man doesn't? And every little mistress with moxie knows how to keep her man up on that phallic pedestal. They tell the story of a very successful—and very hip—French courtesan who was asked the secret of her success. Her reply was classic: "I treat a man as if the sun shines from his backside." So make no mistake. We know what you want. Press the right buttons and we will deliver. The most important button, as if you didn't know, is labeled SEDUCTION.

I recall a quote I ran across somewhere in my indiscriminate reading to the effect, "Seduction is for sissies; a he-man likes his rape." O.K., it's good for a laugh. But the only guy who takes it seriously has to be some variety of sickie. And the gal who believes it has to be the gal who has slept only with such sickies. *Seduction* is, without question, at least in the thinking of this gal (and I know many of my sex who agree with me), the most masculine of the masculine skills. It really should be taught in our schools. Perhaps boys could major in it in college. It might even be introduced to replace R.O.T.C.—"Johnny, get your gun —in bed with Mary!"

Alas, I'm not writing a textbook or teaching a two-semester course. But perhaps I can offer an abbreviated survey of seduction—a sort of guideline to how to make Mary, or Jane, or Sue. For you, lover, it may be only a refresher course. You may have learned the score for scoring with a girl long ago. But stick around. There may be a few things you've forgotten. We all tend, at times, to get careless and out of practice.

Seduction comes in all sizes (and no, that isn't what I meant so don't feel threatened). There is the small-time seducer. He favors the one-two approach—1. tell her you can't live without her; 2. slip your hand inside her panties and agitate. He flubs it with all but the most desperate damsel (and she doesn't need any turn on; she's perpetually horny enough to find *Little Women* a racy novel). And there is the master lover. He might not be able to make it with the mother superior, the coach of the girl's softball team, and the female labor leader—but he makes it two out of three. And what does he do different from the small-timer? Simple. He pays attention to the details. He makes seduction a science. An art. An avocation. And a sport for very grown-up boys and girls.

The master lover plans and works ahead. He knows that seduction isn't a five-minute—or even a one-hour —affair. Timing is important. In fact, timing is the first rule of the game.

You crawl out of bed in the morning. Head all filled with dust, a mouth that tastes like the bottom of a bird cage, and more interest in coffee than the warm feminine body that shared your bed. You grumble as you scrape the hair off your face, and if she's lucky, you grunt, "Good morning." That may be just about the last word she gets out of you until you give her a quick peck as you dash out the door. You bury yourself in the morning paper and for all you seem to care, she could fall through the floor while frying your bacon.

She doesn't hear from you all day. You just don't have time to phone, do you? Do you really believe she buys that "I didn't have a free minute all day" line? She must do something during the day, but do you ever think of what she's doing when you are taking your morning coffee break? And during the hours you are apart, do you ever make plans for the evening with her? I don't mean just on those nights you plan to take her out. What about plans for a romantic evening at home? I know that planning an evening at home would never occur to most husbands. They have the idea that a great sex-filled evening just comes along spontaneously like a winning number on a roulette wheel. Well, I have news for them: the odds against it happening that way on any particular evening are just about the same odds you'll find in playing a number on the wheel. If that's good enough for you, go to it. But scoring consistently with that woman of yours calls for the same careful planning I talked about earlier in discussing dating.

Typical Elmer, the average husband, arrives home at night just about as he was when he left that morning. Sparkling conversation, amorous embrace, and all. He has pulled his necktie down an inch or two on the way. Great ploy. It tells her he's had an incredibly hard day at the office (poor little boy, come let me rub your head). He makes the grand entrance with the usual plastic expression and the typical flat-head conversation: "Hi. How was your day? Anything in the mail?" He shares the latest moves in the office games; she tells him of the current neighborhood gossip and the children's misbehaviors. Exciting? Boy! Clap hands!

He burps his way through dinner and then leaves her to clean the kitchen while he falls asleep over *Tuesday Night at the Movies.* But the best is yet to come, isn't it? Lover boy turns off the tube and climbs into bed beside his woman. She may be half asleep by then, but not for long. Within two minutes she's being poked in the lower back by what feels like a broomstick. Elmer has a hard-on! And she's supposed to be ripe and raunchy. The considerate clod may even give her sixty seconds before "favoring" her with his "let's get down to business" virility. Good old hard-working Elmer can't understand why she isn't passionately pawing him at once, and why, when he slips his hands down between the sheets, he finds things as dry as a desert gopher hole.

Most guys have heard and read about this business called *foreplay* and how important it is supposed to be to a woman. Well, it is. By the way the sex books describe it, you can stick it in your ear for all the good it does a gal. They make it sound as if the secrets to feminine response are found in rubbing, stroking, pinching her in the right places for a few minutes of "warming up." Rub her breasts, titillate her clitoris, and in sixty seconds go! go! go! Those kinds of books just have to be written by flunked-out males who are married to very bored-in-bed females.

All the rubbing, stroking, pinching, licking, biting, etc., etc., etc., is mighty important. Don't ever forget it. *Please!* But it is important to a gal's *satisfaction*— not her *seduction*. A man has to seduce her first before she has much interest in having him begin to do all those finger exercises. Seduction doesn't *start* in bed or when you slip off your shorts to reveal what a treat you have in store for her. In fact, seduction doesn't *start*. If it pays off, it goes on just about all the time. (Yeah, even in your sleep!)

Let me see if I can spell out just what I mean: Since seduction is the highest form of salesmanship, as every sharp salesman knows, *image* is a big, big part of putting the product across. You want her sold on you as the most desirable god-like stud in fifteen counties, if not the world. Your image, then, has to be one of *sexiness*. It is not something you turn on and turn off. The sexy male (or, for that matter, the sexy female) exudes lustiness from every pore at all times. That means he communicates that SEX is never entirely out of his mind.

Do you think that is what some gals complain of when they say, "He only has one thing on his mind"? It isn't, unless the gal has such sex hang-ups she can be recruited to run around pasting fig leaves on statues. Any normal grown-up girl likes knowing her man wakes up in a condition which makes it hard for him to conceal his manhood, and that his mind is hooked up with his glands all day long. *But!* And this is a very important *but:* She wants it all directed toward her. What does she get out of spending that hour or two with eye liner, skin lotions, and exercise if he acts as if any old port in a storm will do? The expert seducer never gives the girl the idea "I need to be laid." His words and action tell her, "I want to make love to *you.*" She's heard these creeps who feel, "If you put a sack over her head, every broad is the same." And her reaction is, "Go do things with yourself in the bathroom, but stay out of my bed."

In the art of seduction, flattery will get you *everywhere.* You start laying the groundwork for seduction with that first morning kiss. Maybe you're not thinking about bedding her right then. You may not even have randy ideas by sundown. But look at it as a long-range investment, a bit like a savings plan. You invest consistently, on a regular basis, and then it's there when you want it. If you don't have it in the savings account, the bank may let you borrow and pay it off in the months to come, but don't expect your woman to live on promises and your good credit. She probably won't go for it. And even if she submits to her 11 P.M. husband with the spur-of-the-moment big ideas, she isn't likely to throw herself into it with the greatest of ardor. The "play with me now and I'll pay with affection later" pitch turns her into a prostitute.

The morning kiss should be a kiss you would never give her mother or your daughter. Imagine you have taken her away for a weekend. You've stopped for dinner at a little place by the ocean with candlelight, a bottle of Chianti, and a guitarist who sings low and soft Italian love songs. Now you take her to a motel. You close the door, slip the night latch, turn, take her in your arms, and kiss her. It's *that* kind of kiss I'm talking about.

Now imagine the following morning. You reach for the phone and order breakfast. When the boy from room service knocks, you have to slip on your trousers quickly (no shorts: you tossed them God-knows-where the night before). She pulls the sheet up around her neck while he places the tray and waits for the tip. Again, you slip the latch on the door and slip off your trousers so the two of you can enjoy a leisurely breakfast *au naturel*. The way you look at her while she pours your coffee. That's the gaze she wants from you in the morning.

When you kiss her good-by and leave her for those long hours of the day, she wants, and for the sake of seduction, she *needs*, to feel you are going to miss her, will be thinking of her, and will be eager to return to her. The message should be: "Damn it! I don't want to have to leave you. I'd much rather take you by the hand back into the bedroom where we could spend the day talking together, laughing together, and playing games of love. Think of me, and thoughts of the evening we'll spend together. You can be sure I'll be thinking of you."

The phone calls during the day should be planned primarily to reinforce the groundwork you have begun. If you must call to ask her to take the car in for an oil change, at least don't start out that way. You're not talking to the garage mechanic. She's your mistress. And in talking with your mistress, one thing should be first in your mind. If it isn't, why do you have a mistress? Why not a housekeeper? Let her know that you are phoning to "touch," to hear the sound of her voice, to say words of love, to tell her you miss her and look forward to taking her in your arms when you walk in the door. She gets busy during the day just as you do. The whole idea is to communicate that no matter how busy you may be, she is still very much in your thoughts—and the thoughts you are having of her make it hard for you to concentrate on anything as dull as the office routine. She may not believe it, but that's all right. She'll get turned on just hearing it.

Gifts are also part of the thinking man's seduction scheme. Provided, that is, they are used to turn her on, not pay her off. The guy who lines up at the candy store on Valentine's Day to buy the same heart-shaped box of chocolates every other congenial Clyde on the block buys his wife isn't the guy who can make a girl dream of sailing the Caribbean with him, two hands on the tiller. The smart seducer thinks in terms of gifts with a message. And the message is always the same: I want *you* to be *my woman*—and I'm going to come on strong to get you. "Seduction gifts" are designed to give the girl "the rush." They keep her "off balance," and that's just where she wants to be—*off balance*. If she's far enough off balance, she'll be flat on her back. Not too bad a position! It doesn't take that much. As the line in the song says, "Little things mean a lot." An "I love you" greeting card. A stock of bedroom incense. A bunch of wild flowers you picked yourself. A scented soap for your shower-à-deux. It isn't the dollar value, but the seduction value, that counts. And let me remind you, lover, seduction gifts are like all other ploys in the seduction game. They should be investments in a *possible* outcome. If they convey, "Here it is; now pay off," they will score a big fat goose egg. If you wait until some afternoon when your palms are

sweaty and your briefs are binding to decide to pick
up a love gift, that *isn't* seduction. It isn't even a prop-
osition. It's an advance payment!

That goes as well for dates. She's not a dummy, you
know. Long before she met you, she probably went
through the experience (and more than a few times)
of dating the big spender who took her out for a great
evening and then screamed like a vaccinated hog if she
didn't come through. If you pull that "I took you out
and tried to show you a good time; now the least you
can do is . . ." nonsense, you deserve a swiftly elevat-
ed knee right below your money belt. Take her out because you want to be out *with her*. And make her
know it. Then, when the time comes for serious seduction, she'll believe you want to make love, not just re-
lieve an ache.

To get down closer to the time of serious seduction:
You walk in the door and you have ideas of testing
out the mattress. If you've built up a good track record with her, you won't surprise her. She'll know that
look in your eye well enough. Greet her in a way that
lets her know how you feel, and what you have been
thinking of, and how eager you have been to be with
her again. Direct your attention and conversation toward her. Keep it centered on her. Take an interest in
her day, in the things which excite her. Notice how she
looks and comment on it. Favorably, of course. If she
has made any changes, whether it be a new shade of
lipstick or a whole new outfit, she wants you to notice
it. If you don't, she may figure you have your mind on
other things, and that's the last thing in the world you
want.

Above all, don't forget physical affection. As if you
could. But that isn't quite what I mean. The physical
down-to-business sex comes later. I'm talking about

touching in a way which tells her you *love* her, not just *want* her. We females, you know, are very "touchy" creatures. We like being touched in a way that expresses your desire for closeness to your woman. When you put your arms around her have it mean something, and I mean something more than, "Take your clothes off." Before the courts gave Hollywood permission to discover the genitals and what we can do with them, the movies used to do a pretty good job with their love scenes. Watch the late shows. What gal wouldn't like her man to play love scenes with her like that? Let the serious sex build up from there. And incidentally, the love-making should be taken seriously when you are showing her affection. That pat-on-the-bottom play is for the clown who pinches girls in elevators when he goes to a sales convention. Believe me, the girl who flips for *that* hasn't been born. Or if she has, I don't want to meet her; she's too much of a dingbat. Somebody should tell some men that slipping a hand under her bra (if she wears one) or up her dress in a "cute" and/or "teasing" way is just about a sure bet to leave her cold—and getting colder. I might as well be the one to tell them, so consider it said.

Providing physical affection can sometimes raise questions of when, where, and how much. If there are just the two of you and no friends or house guests around, from the time you walk through the front door, it can and should be a matter of "let your urges be your guide." But if children are around or you have been invaded by a plague of in-laws, a romp on the living room floor five minutes after you pull in the driveway is going to expell you from the social ball park. Women, at least most women, have a way of getting more uptight over this than men. She may enjoy it when you pat her on the fanny, but not when you're standing in line for the theater. And being nuzzled in her cleavage may be something she waits all day for, but not when she has children running through the room. Maybe some men like to prove their woman is their woman to the whole wide world by a public laying on of hands, but they might stop and consider who they want to impress. Physical affection is supposed to be an act of love. If it embarrasses the gal, how loving can it be?

I'm not saying *any* display of affection around others is a "no-no." Lovers not only *have* more fun, they *are* more fun. Only the most constipated puritan clucks his false teeth when he sees lovers embrace. And the mother who wants to shield her children from the physical affection she shares with their father probably doesn't want to share much with him even when they are alone. She just uses her kids for a cop-out for her own locked-in lack of feeling. I'd draw the line at heavy making-out in front of the children just as I don't go for going two-thirds of the way in a corner booth of a restaurant or riding on a subway. But showing that daddy loves mommy and that they enjoy holding each other, kissing, saying the words of love, is very much what I believe a child should see. If they saw more of it, maybe there wouldn't be so many unhappy, torn-up, children.

The physical affection shouldn't be a stop-on-the-way-through routine bestowed on her for thirty seconds or so as you come in the door, anymore than you should turn it on just fifteen minutes before you hope to score. If you walk in, passionately kiss and embrace her, then go off to your newspaper or martini, she will quickly get wise to the game—"Give her a few gumdrops; you can cash in later." She's waited for you; the day has been a long one. She's been eager for the sound of your voice, the touch of your hands. Now you are home. Show her you've missed her too. *Talk* with her. *Listen* to what she has to say. And *lavish* her with affection. Think about that word *lavish* for a minute. It makes me think of being bathed all over in some luxurious essence, and that's the feeling a woman wants from the affection her man gives her.

If you have children in the house, the situation calls for diplomacy. Later on, I'll have some things to say about how to keep a love affair going and growing with other people constantly in the picture, but for now let me just say that she was there before they were and if you want to keep her your woman, make very sure she knows she is still number one when it comes to your attention. Kids can be extremely demanding and self-centered. When daddy walks in the door, they may knock one another to the floor getting to him, and mother may be one of the first to be shoved out of the way. She may even have conflicts in her role of "good mother" and feel the children deserve the attentions of their father even if it means that she goes wanting. If she does, and she isn't willing or able to fight for her rights to her man, that is where you step in. Let your progeny know, in no uncertain terms, that she comes first. They can wait. This popular notion that children have some deep-seated, insatiable need to climb all over their father as soon as he walks through the door, and that a "good" father must drop everything and ignore his woman, leaving her in the kitchen to prepare the food for the tribe while he runs romper room in another part of the house, is psychological guano. If she is the one pushing this "You go play with the children; they've missed you and need their father" gospel, you may have some straightening out to do. Patiently explain the basic facts of a love af-

fair to her. That she is the gal you want an affair with
and this means you intend keeping her first. The kids
will get more than enough of your attention *after* you
have had the chance to be with her, just the two of
you. You weren't father and mother when you started
your affair, and you will have no chance of any affair
continuing if you become "Dad" and "Mom" in the
way you see each other. Regardless of what the amateur head-shrinkers of the PTA crowd say (and you
can bet they all wear flannel nightgowns), no child
ever feels rejected because his parents have a great
thing going between them and intend to keep it that
way.

I said if you have a good track record with her she
will know what you have in mind at all times. The
perceptive mistress, living with an attentive lover, is
able to pick up the clues in the morning that that coming evening will be a beautiful adventure—even before
he knows it. But that isn't to say the female of the
species is endowed with clairvoyance. Maybe you
think you're throwing out the messages, but either because your throwing arm is poor or she isn't looking in
the right way or the right place, she isn't catching
them. The idea of the seduction game is to *prepare* the
gal for the love-making to come. It's one area of your
affair where "surprises" often bomb. Communication
is too important to a love affair to take chances. If
you have feelings in that direction when you talk to
her on the phone in the afternoon, let her know it. She
may have a dozen things happening right then and another dozen on her mind. If you don't let her know
what you have on *your* mind for later on, it may work
to the disadvantage of both of you. You don't have to
make it a flat statement of intent: "Tonight's the
night." Remember, love and romance, to a woman,

should carry a flavor of subtlety. You can get the message across very clearly by suggesting, "Why don't we take our shower early tonight and have a nice long evening?" Those little "hints" dropped during the evening as well as earlier in the day help turn her thinking on to what you want her thinking of. If, at four o'clock in the afternoon, she is tipped off to what you have in mind for later and this starts her motor running down the same track, by nine o'clock that evening when the two of you climb in the shower, you can look forward with confidence to great things ahead.

CHAPTER FIVE

The Where
and When of It

For years now I've heard about making it while swinging from the chandelier, and I'll admit I get some kick from the visual image it produces, but my image keeps crashing head on with my practical side. Who climbs up on the chandelier? Both? What kind of contortions do they employ? And what do they do when the chandelier comes crashing to the floor? Continue amidst the broken glass and shattered light bulbs?

So all right! I'm willing to try something new. A new way, in a new place. I just don't know about the swinging from the ceiling bit. But if it can be done, fine. It may have a few innovations to offer. The point to be considered is one of what can be done to break the boredom of sex, or prevent its occurrence.

Yes, I did say boredom. And I hate even to mention the word in relationship to something as much fun as sex. But I might as well admit it, and you might as well too. Sex *can* become a big fat bore. Those porno novels where all the boys in the fraternity line up to take their turn in a gang-bang with the town chippie always make the gal out to be consumed in a fit of sexual frenzy. Maybe it's a good thing it is fiction. If it ever occurred in real life and someone were to ask the girl how she felt, her answer might clobber the fragile male ego. By college boy number three, she would be more than a little annoyed that he and his chums were keeping her awake! Sex is a little like a good steak or an afternoon at the circus. It's delicious and exciting, but how many times can you repeat it the same way and remain turned on. Answer: Not long.

Homo Sapiens are the only members of the animal kingdom capable of boredom. I have a German shepherd who goes on, month after month, apparently relishing the same prepared dog food. He never lets me know by his lack of interest that he had the same dish of kibbles the evening before and would like a change of diet, just for variety. But what if that gal of yours served you a top sirloin twice a day? Even if you were mad for steak, in a few days you would most likely turn on her and take to eating in a coffee shop. The same goes for sex. Keep it boxed in to a late night, lights-out, in-bed ritual and something or someone not far away may begin to look mighty appealing. We've all heard it said that men are polygamous by nature, that they are simply *never* satisfied with a single woman in their life. Before they ever escape their teens, girls are told, repeatedly, and usually by embittered house fraus, that no man can be expected to remain faithful. So up they climb on their little crosses of cynicism and femaleness to spit down venomous spitballs of hatred toward the world of lecherous males.

For the women who read this book, they will be

happy to know I am not going to let the men off the
hook on this one. I am convinced men are continually
seeking variety in their partners. The gal who offers a
new approach and promises a novel experience can do
to males what catnip does to cats—and then some.
What most men don't know, and few women will admit, is that this applies every bit as much to us gals.
We also get bored making love to the same man in the
same way. The woman who claims she doesn't like a
variety of lovers either doesn't dig sex at all or isn't
very given to the truth.

This doesn't mean she has a penchant for sexual
hopscotch, jumping from bed to bed. I don't care what
any of the "swingers" say, the guy or gal who changes
partners like he or she would change a flash bulb isn't
chasing after sex, he is pursuing a neurosis—and the
neurosis is winning! An adult male with the right quo-
ta of virility and imagination can transform himself
into thirteen different lovers, and he can entice his
woman into being twenty-six different courtesans. If
anyone wishes to figure out the number of possible
combinations to that, do let me know.

Needless to say, a big part of what it takes to be
thirteen different lovers rests in love-making technique, of which I'll have something to say later. A major contribution, however, comes from the setting of
love. A couple *could* have sex in the steam room of
the YMCA, on a morgue slab, or in a jail cell, but unless they have gone without it for a month or so, the
experience won't have much to offer. The "essentials"
would be present, but that would be all, a little like
eating a gourmet meal on a card table in your garage.
When you make love, and *where* you make love are
just about as big in determining your success as *how*

you make love—at least as far as a woman is concerned.

First, the *when* of it:

As just about anyone with a serious interest in sex will agree, most people have sex at all the wrong times. Maybe not the *wrong* times, but certainly not the *best* times. I don't know that anyone has made a study of it, but my guess is that ninety per cent or more of the times most couples have sex is late at night after everything and anything else has been done. They've eaten a full meal, cleaned up the kitchen, read the newspaper, helped the kids with their homework, discussed the family budget, and stared at the tube for three hours. *Then* they fall into bed and have five or ten minutes of sex, followed at once by snoring. Think about it for a minute: Sex calls for energy. And in any single day, we only have so much energy and no more. I don't care how many ideas you may have, if you're simply beat at the end of the day, your body isn't going to go along with you. I hate to be critical of men, but I believe many males approach sex as a sort of afterthought. Most men have an erection when they wake up, but they don't have thoughts of sex, or if they do, they suppress them, climb out of bed and go off to the bathroom. The guy showers in the morning, but not in the evening when he takes his gal to bed. He shaves, dresses, gulps his coffee, and races off to work. After a full day of doing whatever he is paid to do, he fights the traffic home, downs his double martini, and five hours later yawns, stretches, and lumbers off to bed. He might want to be the great lover when he gets there, but he will do well if he can just keep it up long enough to perform at all. And how

responsive is his partner going to be if she is thinking
of how early she has to get up and how late it is?

Those Latin countries have the right idea. The men
come home for a couple of hours siesta in the afternoons. They say the siesta is taken up with eating a
big meal and perhaps grabbing a short nap to let it settle, but they're not fooling this gal. I know they are
not spending all that time eating chili rellenos. Until
we become civilized enough to introduce the siesta to
our rush-rush society, however, the afternoon of loving will, for most of us, have to be limited to weekends
and vacations. Ah, but don't overlook those weekends,
days off, overnight shackups, and vacations for two.
They offer time for loving when you are not faced
with limits and fatigue. A Saturday afternoon can be
spent more profitably than in doing the yard work and
cleaning the garage. If you don't think the bedroom
offers superior possibilities, all I can ask is, "When
did you join the ranks of the aged and infirm?" If your
gal doesn't prefer the loving to the laundry, take a
two-step approach: 1. Check out your abilities as a
lover, and 2. If you are doing everything a red-blooded girl could desire, check her out to find out what to
do to get her motor running.

Saturday and Sunday mornings when you have no
clock to watch are great. The coffee maker can be
placed on the night stand ready to be plugged in. You
can add a bowl of fruit, maybe even some breakfast
rolls, and you're set for a timeless morning limited
only by imagination and desire—with all the well-rest-
ed energy needed to meet both.

"That's fine so long as you don't have children," is
going to be the answer of more than a few of you
reading these suggestions. To which I say, "Do some
rethinking on that one." Take the matter of a Saturday

afternoon "siesta." If the kids are older, that is, not pre-schoolers, they don't need their parents present each and every minute. They can be outside playing with their friends or watching television or whatever. If they have a habit of pounding on the door whenever the two of you try to be alone, it's time you break them of the habit before you develop the urge to break their little necks. If they are pre-school age, it can be even easier: put them down for a nap. They are often more agreeable to napping if they know Daddy and Mommy are also going to be "napping." If it still doesn't work out well, or if you want the freedom of more rooms than just the bedroom, try getting a neighborhood girl to baby-sit with them at the park for a couple of hours or so. What better investment can *you* think of?

The mornings in bed may present another problem. Children have a way of wanting to be fed the minute they open their eyes, and they usually are not long on patience. O.K., but if there are older children, they can take over the breakfast once in a while. If there are only young ones, what's wrong with getting up and feeding them, then going back to bed while they watch the Saturday morning cartoons? The "good mother" types will never go for it, but then, they emotionally dropped their men with the first pregnancy anyway. They wouldn't have it any different.

Vacations, of course, offer the ultimate freedom of time where loving is concerned. With a big *IF*. If you make it a vacation just for two, without friends along, without visits to relatives, without new-found acquaintances you met the evening before and promised to meet for tennis or brunch, and without the children. (And for the record, *NO* I am not suggesting parents should not take their children on vacations, only that they also plan vacations for the two of them—even if only for overnight and a day.) And *if* you don't jam the vacation with all kinds of sight-seeing and other plans which get the two of you out of the room early in the A.M. and keep you on the run all day. Those *bags-in-the-lobby-and-on-the-bus-at-7:30* A.M. conducted-tour vacations may be ginger peachy to the camera nuts, but for lovers they miss by a mile. The two things above all else a vacation for two should provide are romance and relaxation—in that order. And a vacation of romance is, by its very nature, relaxing. What could be more luxurious than an afternoon of love-making in a hotel room in which you have the time to doze off afterward and awaken later to dress for a late supper for two, or perhaps call room service and dine in the room?

Love-making in the morning or afternoon has another advantage: daylight. Since our first experiences in love-making were generally at night, in the dark, and we go on, perhaps out of necessity, due to working hours, having sex after the lights are out, we begin to think of it as the only "normal" time for it. Or, we simply fall into the sex-in-the-dark rut. I've talked to many gals who find love-making by daylight particularly exciting. The obvious plus to it is the opportunity to view one another clearly. Women enjoy the expression which comes over a man's face when he looks at their physical charms. As I mentioned before, we're vain creatures. And it goes without saying that any woman who is turned on to sex at all is stimulated by viewing the nude body of her lover.

Of course, if you do make love at night, there is nothing that says you must turn off the lights. Which brings me to the matter of setting for sex.

If a couple average twice a week for sex, you can

bet they will double or triple their average if they spend a week in a hotel or motel, and it isn't all simply a matter of having more time. There is something about a motel room which causes our thoughts to turn lightly to thoughts of using the mattress for a trampoline for two. Maybe it brings back memories of illicit nights. There is always a delightful naughtiness in shacking-up. But there is another reason, one having to do with what I said about sexual boredom.

Most of us can't shack up in a motel every night, and even if we could, that would undoubtedly become a bore in time. It's the variety which defeats boredom. So how do you break boredom in the setting of a home you've lived in for months or years? To be honest, lover, it takes imagination. But imagination doesn't cost much, and the rewards make it worth it.

To begin with, sex in the bedroom has become almost a fixation. That's where the bed is, but who says that sex always has to be in bed? If it can be accomplished on horseback (and it can!), or done in a swimming pool (which is truly refreshing!), it can be adapted to any room in the house (excluding closets, which offer little I can think of). A living room can be great. If you have a fireplace, what can enhance skin tones more than firelight? And the warmth of a fire on bare skin is a sensuous experience comparable to a needle shower or satin sheets. Making love on the floor is, in itself, a different experience from sex in bed. If your floor is carpeted, the texture of the carpet along your body can be a turn-on. Even a bare floor can provide a different sort of kick. The firmness of a floor allows a very different movement from a bed, especially suited for those times when she wants to be "taken" by a lover who "rapes" her. If you have a stereo in the living room, so much the better. You can put on a sensuous record, turn up the volume, and *feel* the vibrations roll over you as you make love. The furniture in a living room also offers many possibilities. The couch is obvious, and it may bring back the romance of pre-married days—remember? The other furniture can be employed in a number of variations in the art of love. Think for a minute of all the ways you can sit, kneel, and even stand in an overstuffed chair. And don't overlook the coffee table. If you can't come up with any ideas for it, perhaps some suggestions in later chapters will make you look at it in a new light.

And how about the kitchen? She spends a lot of her time there doing a lot of mundane tasks. Suppose the kitchen held memories of something more than dirty dishes and potato peelings. It might take some of the household doldrums away and keep you in her thoughts while she shoves the peelings down the disposal and scrapes away at a burned pan. Now there is no law says you can't make love on the kitchen floor, but there are other possibilities for which the kitchen is ideally suited. Take the kitchen table, for example. Oral sex with one of you seated at the table while the partner lies back across the table, feet dangling, is just one possibility. Think of the memories you will have of the very special dessert she served you!

The bathroom, of course, offers the special advantages to be found in bathing together. Some limited thinkers will say a bathtub is not adaptable for two, but they're wrong (unless, of course, you're both slightly huge). Seated positions for sex can be lots of fun in a full tub of warm water with bath oil added. And it goes without saying that showers are built for two. Sex in a shower may be limited to the preliminaries and mutual arousal of washing each other all over, but sex all the way is far from out of the question. Not only are standing positions fun with the shower peppering your skin, think of the possibilities if you take the kitchen stool into the shower.

You see what I mean when I say don't rule out *any* room in the house? Even the laundry room shouldn't be ruled out. Sitting her up on top of the washing machine while the machine is running and you are doing nice things to her with your lips and hands may sound pretty kinky, but have you ever felt the vibrations of that machine?

Unless you are absolutely a nut on variety in your love-making locale, however, you will probably, like the rest of us, have sex in the bedroom more often than elsewhere. Since it is the most frequented setting for sex, it makes utmost good sense to do everything you can to make it an atmosphere conducive, even stimulating, to sex. On this score, most bedrooms just don't make it at all. Those bedrooms they photograph for the home magazines must be decorated by the same types who design women's clothes. Sexy they are *not!* The rooms are cluttered with ruffles and chintz and stuffed toys or else they look as antiseptically "modern" as a surgical theater. They are every bit as exciting as the art reproductions in your dentist's office. Fine, if you want to sleep and nothing else. Do you suppose they're all decorated by frigid housewives or Seventh Avenue gays?

Unless you dig celibacy, everything, and I do mean *everything*, in the décor of your bedroom should be conducive to *sex*. The colors, the lighting, the furnishings, the decorations. *Everything*. Start with the bed since that's where most of the action is. Until recently, there wasn't much one could do with a bed except try to find one that didn't leave you with an aching back.

But now modern science and ingenuity have given us the best thing to happen to sex since they learned to pick the locks on chastity belts: *the water bed.* Whoever the ad man was who said there are two things better on a water bed and one of them is sleeping surely knew what I'm talking about. If you haven't, you'll have to take my word for it. The sensation defies description. The closest I can come is to say that stretching out on a water bed is a little like reclining on one of those inflated rafts in a swimming pool. You move in any direction and the waves begin. Dig your feet in or press down with your elbows and the gentle waves sweep back and forth under you. With more active movement, hang on and enjoy a great ride! Water beds are also imminently practical. The mattress will never get lumpy, and if it finally gets too many leaks to patch, it can be replaced for very little. Also, the initial price is no higher than a conventional mattress and box spring, much less for the basic models. The big thing is what it does for your love life. I don't know whether the small towns in Nebraska have them yet, but when they do, count on the corn country to offer something more to do on a summer evening than watch the fireflies.

Water bed or no, two other things add to the sexual utility of a bed: extra pillows and satin sheets. The extra pillows speak for themselves. Propping up on a pillow can add something extra to various positions. As for the satin sheets, they are simply delectable. Nothing except your lover's skin is as nice to rub against. (We have another added "special" on our water bed: an imitation seal skin fur bedspread that has a feel that's out of this world!)

I think if I could have only one room in the house carpeted, I would choose the bedroom, and it would be a nice deep pile carpeting. Not only is it nice on the feet when you climb out of bed, it provides yet another fun locale for amorous pursuits. And incidentally, I think carpeting in the bathroom is the ultimate in luxury, but then I'm a creature of self-indulgent comfort as well as sensualism.

You can also add a lot to the bedroom by giving thought to the lighting. There is no reason why bedroom lighting has to be plain old white bulbs. If you keep a couple of extra bulbs, maybe blue and amber, in the night stand drawer, you can change the entire atmosphere of your love hideaway with a simple change of color. By blue or amber light, she can become an excitingly new person to you. And it can produce a similar effect for her. Candlelight is also a fun illumination in the bedroom. Anyone looks better by candlelight, and what better time to look your best?

Before we reluctantly move on from the topic of bedroom décor, one more suggestion: Mirrors do wonders in transforming a bedroom from a room to sleep in to a room designed for romance. Love-making reflected in a mirrored wall or ceiling is, as many of the world's great loving couples will attest, an expanding experience. Don't ask me why. Maybe we're all narcissists at heart. Those mirror tiles can be purchased by the box, and easily applied with a double tape. You can mirror an entire wall and/or ceiling in an afternoon and still be rested up enough to test out the effect that evening. About now, you may be saying, "Yeah, but I don't have anything to do with furnishing the bedroom. She is the one in charge of that, and what if she doesn't go along with all this?" That, lover, is where that salesmanship comes in again. If she can be shown how an improved décor, one more conducive to romance, will add new dimensions to her days and nights with you, what right-thinking gal would resist?

Being a nature lover, I must put in a strong plug for the great outdoors as a setting for love-making. Granted the outdoors isn't what it used to be and it is becoming a frantic frustration to find *anyplace* where you can get away from the maddening throng. Obviously, the Yosemite National Park during the summer is not the place to make mad love under a spreading tree. You'd be stepped on by twelve Boy Scouts before being run over by a camp trailer. Nevertheless, if you live anywhere but New York or Los Angeles or some equally wretched urban sprawl, you probably can find some hidden-away spots with trees, lakes, streams, or an ocean. Why not a picnic for two? A bottle of chilled wine, a salami, and fresh fruit are enough. And of course, don't forget to bring along a blanket and perhaps a pillow. You might even include a good book to read together—like maybe one from your collection of erotica.

Naturally, the first thing one thinks about in such situations is, "What if somebody were to come along?" Well, I'm assuming none of us is going to try making out in a pasture fifty feet from a freeway interchange. You search around until you find a secluded spot. If it isn't littered with beer cans, you can be pretty sure you won't be bothered. There are even beaches left which come close to what you might find on a desert island, but the last one in this country may have disappeared by the time this is in print. Even so, if you are an ocean buff, and who isn't, you can spend loving evenings on a beach that is less than overrun with surfers and bonfires. A couple of sleeping bags zipped together will keep you snug, close, and private. And what better backdrop for romance could you ask than the sound of the waves and the silver sparkle of phosphorescence on the water?

You've selected the best time, and the most conducive setting. Now, it's up to you. So on to the next steps . . .

CHAPTER SIX

The How of It:
Twoplay

Think about sex and you think about a naked man and a naked woman and a rather astounding variety of things they can do to and for each other. Right? Well you shouldn't. The perspective is too narrow. Sex doesn't start with the clothes off unless you are nudists or simply want to eliminate everything but the essentials—romance included. Love-making, under all but unusual circumstances, should start with the clothes on, not off. This isn't a matter of prudish modesty. When it comes to sex, clothes are there to be taken off. But not right from the start.

Of course you can always go off to the bedroom, take off your clothes, and drop them over the chair while your woman is brushing her teeth, disrobing, and winding the alarm clock. Then both of you can climb into bed and turn out the light. And finally, you can reach out to touch each other, usually with a good night kiss. You *can* do that, but you lost about twelve per cent of the potential kicks. Undressing each other is one of the nicest steps in the building ascent of love-making. In it, the one thing the undressing of the other says, in effect, "I'm turned on by you and by your body and I want to be able to enjoy the sight of it." The one being undressed communicates a surrender to the loved one, saying, "I have a gift for you and I'll let you unwrap it."

But before the undressing, reverence her body. Touch her. Explore her features with your fingertips as one blind might seek to read the features of a rediscovered friend. Run your fingers slowly through the hair of her temples, brushing your fingertips lightly about her ears and to the nape of her neck. Draw your fingers, ever so lightly, over the skin of her cheeks, the corners of her mouth, her eyelids. Move your fingers over her skin slowly, in a caress, carefully and lovingly, with a touch something like the touch you might employ in examining a highly polished surface with the sensitive tips of your fingers. Your touch should not only give tactual pleasure to her, it should clearly communicate your pleasure in the touching. Like all loving, it should have a timelessness in it. If it has in it any suggestion of impatience, any hint of hurrying on to the next step in love-making, it will be a failing gesture. There is a lot of the feline in every woman. We like being petted, caressed, made to purr with the deep satisfaction of being spoiled with love. Few gals I know would ever complain of too much of such tender treatment at the hands of a lover.

Kissing is something which deserves perhaps a chapter of its own. From my own observations, I long ago concluded that a lover's kiss, like most other acts of love, carries a greater impact for women than for men. How did I reach this conclusion? Simple. If men got as much from it, there would be a lot more kissing going on—several times over. And it would become a much more highly developed art form.

A woman's lips most certainly qualify as one of the most erogenous spots on her body. The gal who can't be highly aroused by a prolonged, deep, and meaningful kiss from her lover probably can't be turned on by anything. But as everyone past the age of fourteen knows, there are kisses *and* there are *kisses*. The kisses we gals are continually craving are those which make us think of nothing but sex, and tell us the men in our lives are thinking of nothing but sex. They are not hello and good-by kisses, paternal kisses, or kisses of gratitude. Save those for your mother. We want to be kissed in a way that will stir all sorts of strong feelings in some private areas of our bodies.

The first rule should be: Turn off everything else when you are kissing her. If that business call you have to make, or the televised football game that's coming on in five minutes, or the overdrawn checking account is bouncing around in your head while you are kissing her, she'll know it, and if it has any sexual affect at all, it will be in the reverse. I don't know how or why when other things are going on a touch changes, but it does. It loses the quality of "oneness" that communicates an aliveness to each other and a caring. No woman wants to compete with other people and things in her man's world when she is kissing and being kissed. She probably would most often rather forget the whole thing. So when you kiss her, focus on *her*. *Her* lips. *Her* tongue. *Her* body. The taste. The fragrance. The warmth of her body. That important other world of yours will still be there waiting an hour or a day later. Shut the door on it when you take her in your arms.

Occasionally, one of those fierce "impassionate" kisses can be exciting. You know the kind, where he grabs her in his arms and "crushes his lips against her." But unless your woman digs such kisses almost exclusively, and most gals don't, most of your kisses should begin slowly, and build from there. *Tenderness* is still the word. Brush her lips with yours. Explore, very delicately, the outline of her lips, first with your lips, then the tip of your tongue. Let her lips yield to yours. Entice her into the response you seek. Note: I didn't say *tease*, although many writers on sex do use that word. Teasing is something we hated our little brothers for doing. A woman wants her lover to enhance and stimulate her appetite, not "tease" her. In kissing her, your tongue draws her inescapably into thoughts of the sex act. The thoughts are simply unavoidable. Your tongue penetrating her lips is your penis penetrating the lips between her legs. The kiss provides a preview of things to come. With your tongue you tell her how you will approach her to enter her body. And it makes her all the more eager for what will follow.

Run the tip of your tongue, and only the tip, lightly and slowly over and around her lips. Not between her lips; not yet. Concentrate. Allow yourself to enter fully into the experience of communicating through the subtle movements of lips and tongue. Don't rush it! I know I've said that before. Forgive me, but it's so important it can never be said too many times. The most satisfying love-making is something like the *1812 Overture;* it builds in a crescendo until, at its peak, cannons fire and the tensions which have been building explode. In love-making, the tensions building are a big, big part of the satisfactions. It's too good ever to rush, especially for a woman. And if you look at it from your standpoint, you have everything to gain by going slow. The more time and care you put into building her fires, the more she will contribute to the explosions when they come. And isn't that what you hope for?

When you penetrate her lips with your tongue, make it a penetration; don't just push your tongue into her mouth. Remember, it is the sex act itself you are stimulating with your tongue entering between her lips. It shouldn't make her think of rape. Let your tongue dart between her lips. Just the tip of your tongue. Penetrate only her lips at first. Your tongue asks for entrance; it doesn't crash through the portals. Let her yield to your request. You'll be able to know it when she does. She may open her mouth fully to accept your tongue, or simply relax her lips to allow you to penetrate them. From there, you can do several things, all of them fun. She may enjoy having you extend your tongue as far as you can, fully into her mouth. With her tongue, she can press it against the roof of her mouth and suck on it hard, like a lollipop. If you don't penetrate as deeply, she can meet your tongue with hers and play delightful games of fun, mutually "pursuing" and touching with your tips, allowing her, if she chooses, to penetrate your mouth with her tongue in a "reversal of roles" which communicates her arousal.

Don't overlook the fact that she has to breathe. Not that you don't, of course, but you are the one assuming the aggressive role in the kissing and sometimes, lover, you may come on strong enough to give a gal the feeling of being smothered or swallowed up. If you have your mouth completely covering hers and don't let up every few seconds, she may come up gasping. If she has the sniffles and can't easily breathe through her nose, you may watch her turn blue. Kissing can go on indefinitely, and why not? Only a few other things you can do will contribute to her arousal quite as much. But if you are to continue the kissing very long, it can be tiring. It won't be if you break off frequently for a breather.

While you are kissing her, you are going to be doing something with your hands. She wants you to make use of them. Use them well, and her response to your kiss will be something you've had far-out dreams about. I know what you'd like to do with your hands. If you led something less than a sheltered childhood, you at least tried doing most of them on high school dates. But at this stage, keep your hand out of her bra and out from under her skirt. Plenty of time for that later. But don't, on the other hand, just bear hug her. You don't have to hang on to her; she doesn't want to run away. Try taking her face tenderly in your hands, lifting it to meet your lips, then running your fingertips over her cheeks, throat, ears, and elsewhere. Or, with your fingers, memorize the curve of her shoulders, the muscles that run alongside her spine, the indentation of her waist. Let your hands roam. Move them up along the outside of her thighs to her waist. Move your fingers over her hips and the cleavage of her buttocks, and in circles at the small of her back, pulling her in against your body.

Your caresses outside her clothing should *promise* what is coming, not deliver it. The more you promise, the more she has to look forward to, and the more she has to look forward to, the more turned on she is bound to become. So make a production of it, lover.

Make her feel she can't wait to shed her clothes and tear yours off. She'll love you for it—and in the best way imaginable.

All those annoying clinical sex manuals devote a page or two to what they like to call foreplay. Yeeech! Rub this, stroke that, press, pinch, or poke something else, and it's supposed to be "Open, Sesame!" They always make a female sound like a combination safe with a half dozen or so added "magic buttons." You can just bet they're written by guys who put women to sleep *before*, not after. I even think that word "foreplay" must have been the invention of a eunuch or a sheep breeder. You don't warm up in some sexual bullpen to get ready for a quick climax. Yet that's the way they make it sound. I have a new word for you: *Twoplay*. There are all kinds of wonderful things you can do for and to each other with all parts of your bodies. And most of them are games which two can play. Hence, my new name for it. For the sake of equality of sex and satisfaction, don't come at us gals with that warm-up approach. We want to be pleasured, and we want to pleasure our men. But we can't do much (or get much) if we know that just as soon as a man hears our first sigh, or after he spends ninety seconds playing with the left breast, or discovers something is moist inside our panty hose, he wants to move in for the finale.

Before you start playing games with your clothes off, try a few more erotic exercises with them on, through them and under them. Did you ask why? It does seem like less than the most convenient approach. Getting a hand down inside a blouse and under a snug-fitting bra may be doing it the hard way at that. And things like ski pants and panty girdles can be as formidable as the Berlin Wall; you can't even be sure what you're touching; it's either memories or an act of faith. Why fool around through the fabrics? A couple of very good reasons: First, it prolongs the games of loving, and anything which can keep the sensual scene going in a way which will draw out a few more earthy feelings deep down has got to be good. And more important, that hand inside her bra and your fingers fumbling with her panties bring back some very exciting memories. Isn't that the way you first made love to her? There was such a delicious wickedness to it then, and she luxuriates in having you recall it with those same talented hands.

She can, needless to say, also make love to you through your clothing. If she doesn't do so on her own, encourage her. Unless she has hang-ups, she will be more than eager to explore that male body of yours. A gal likes verifying with her fingers the effect she has had on her man. She just might, however, hold back out of fear of being "forward," and the old mystique that says sex is solely a masculine pursuit. In the beginning, she may need your encouragement. If there are places you would like her hands, take them in yours and place them there. You know what will make you feel good. Share it with her.

If the time is now right for disposing of clothes, make an art of it. Which means, in a word, make love to her while you disrobe her. The order in which you divest her of her raiment will, of course, be partly determined by what she is wearing. Some clothes, sorry to say, call for help from the gal, but most things can be very nicely handled by a man. The rule for stripping a girl is very simple: Continue to turn her on while you do it. Let's suppose she has on an outfit that's very easy to take off, a skirt and blouse. You can start with the blouse. O.K., maybe you've unbuttoned a girl's blouse a hundred or more times, but have you ever tried to make the removal of a blouse an erotic act in itself? It sure can be. Believe me!

You might try it something like this: Instead of moving straight down the row of buttons, one, two, three, four, open just the top two or three. And pause. Make love to the part of her body you have uncovered. Move your fingertips over her shoulders. Brush her skin with your lips. Having her man make love to her shoulders is something no woman ever tires of. The nape of the neck, like the ears, is a special turn-on area for many gals. If you haven't discovered this with your gal, try it. Five to one it sends shivers all the way down her spine.

Try slipping your hand inside her bra before you go about taking it off. You want to increase her eagerness to have it off. By beginning your caresses before removing her bra, you help build the tension of anticipation for both of you. When you do help her shed the bra and blouse, go slow. Don't go at her like a lion after a slab of raw meat at feeding time. Those sex manuals usually present a step-one, step-two, step-three approach. First, you're told to kiss her, then stimulate her breasts, then move to her genitals. The order is unvarying, and step one is forgotten once step two is commenced. As a technique, it doesn't make it, at least not with our sex. Don't stop the kissing and the fingertips through her hair and the light caresses to her cheeks and throat just because you have her stripped to the waist and now have something else to play with. The varied stimulations of love-making should always *expand* to include more, not drop one thing and "move on" to another. Hold her, press her breasts against you; kiss her.

And don't forget our female vanity and all the

things I said about a gal's insecurity where her bust line is concerned. Compliment her on what you see. Tell her how much you love the size and shape of them. I don't care how many times you may have told her in the past, she won't stop you from saying it again. When it comes to her breasts, there are some things about the female sexual anatomy which every man should know. You've probably discovered quite a bit about it by trial and error, and some of the errors may have amounted to strike-outs (just one more reason why they should have compulsory classes in love-making). The breasts are classed as primary erogenous areas of a gal's body. Of course, nobody ever says what this is supposed to mean. Well let me tell you what it means to me, and, from what other women have said, to probably the majority of women. It means that there are only a couple of other places you can caress which will do the same delightful things to us. Some of us can even reach orgasm just by prolonged stimulation of our nipples. I think it would happen to more of my sex if their men could learn a little more about what feels best. Those dumb books usually tell the guy to stimulate the woman's breasts or to "play" with them. That helps like nothing at all. A swat with a ping-pong paddle is "stimulation." And bouncing them back and forth like a pair of handballs might be considered playful. But if you try either technique, she just might retaliate in similar fashion to *your* most vulnerable spot. So the first rule should be: Take it easy. A brisk rubdown or a deep massage is *not* a caress, and when it comes to her breasts, the emphasis should always be on caressing. Be gentle. Approach them with consideration. *Love* them. And don't stop showing her—with your words, hands, and lips—how much you enjoy them.

Second rule: Don't start with the nipples. Make her wait and want for it. The more her passion is permitted to climb gradually, the higher it will be when she reaches her peak. Her nipples, as I'm sure you learned long ago, are just about as erotically sensitive as her clitoris. Well, maybe not quite; but almost. If you start with your lips and tongue on her nipples, you're forcing her to leap to the top of the mountain in a single jump. Try brushing your fingers down from her armpits under the curve of her breast. Move them in light circling caresses over the surface of each breast, touching lightly the pigmented area (areola). But not yet the nipples. Cup them in your hands, lifting them, moving and pressing them in a slow, gentle, loving "massage." Run your lips and tongue over the same route, in circles that approach, but don't include, those waiting nipples. Press your lips into her cleavage while you cup her breasts against your cheeks. When you've gone that far for a while, stop! Don't go on to her nipples right away. Catch up on the kisses and caresses before returning to her breasts. In each thing you do, always leave her aching for more of the same.

When you first stimulate her nipples, do it with your lips and tongue, not with your fingers. This isn't a hard and fast rule, but there is a reason for it. The nipples are very sensitive and they can easily get sore. Your lips and tongue are probably less coarse and sandpapery than your fingers and your tongue can lubricate her nipples with saliva to reduce the friction. Don't get me wrong. I'm not saying a gal wants a man with rose petal hands. She likes those masculine hands of yours. But if she gets sore nipples, then that part of the fun may have to end, and that would be a shame. Following our basic rule of don't give her everything at once, be very miserly with the use of your tongue on her nipples . . . You don't want to spoil her—quite yet. Flick your tongue over and around one nipple two or three times. Then move to the other one. Place your lips over it in a light kiss and move the tip of your tongue rapidly back and forth and up and down. Try lightly squeezing her nipple between your lips. Some sexperts suggest gently biting the nipples, and I'll admit it can turn a gal on, but I must say the guy better know what he's doing, and she better have a lot of confidence that he does. It's a little like those circus acts where the elephant is trained to suspend his front foot a few inches over the trainer's head. A little too much, and it can be downright painful.

That goes as well for other things you do to her. Almost all women enjoy having their nipples sucked. Maybe it makes them feel sort of maternal, but why analyze: it feels oh so good! The whole idea should be to let her responses be your guide. When you take her nipple in your mouth, you might, for example, try gently rolling it with your tongue against the back of your teeth or the roof of your mouth. If it feels good to her, you'll know it from her reactions. Hang on to the information; it will come in handy in the future.

You may have read that the nipples become erect when she is aroused. Those Victorian porno novels always made a big thing of protruding nipples on their perpetually turned on nymphs. One more contribution to the sexual confusion. Yes, the nipples do become firm and "erect" in most women under sexual stimulation, but don't use it as a measure of how much she is turned on. In the first place, women vary in this response just as they vary in size and shape of their breasts and nipples. The gal with very small nipples might have the "telltale response" without you even being aware of it. For another thing, the response doesn't always occur. Or at least not to the same degree, even though she might be just as turned on one time as another. Furthermore, they may become erect while you are kissing or otherwise doing nice things to them but then lose their erection without it indicating she is any less hot and eager. So forget it. No gal likes to have her responses evaluated and recorded like a blood-pressure reading. It tells her that her lover is insecure. And makes her feel like a bug in a laboratory.

Now I'm going to make a great big digression which isn't a digression at all. I want to talk about one of the nicest things that can happen to a girl, for that matter, to a man also. *A massage.*

I don't know who the first man was who gave a massage to his woman, but if she blabbed to the other girls about it (the little ninny), I'll bet she had to fight off her competition with clubs and stones. I can picture the scene: Our caveman has dragged his woman by the hair, home to the cave. Her tiger-skin sarong is worn fur-bare by the rocky terrain, and she has sore spots in areas the sun seldom touched. Her humor was rubbed as raw as her backside. Then our muscle man got stricken with a sharp pang of conscience and compassion (or maybe he saw his chances of scoring that evening quickly going down the tubes). He waited until she stretched out on her tummy. Then he began rubbing her where he thought she had the fewest bruises: across the shoulders. She probably tried to stay mad at him, but by the time he had worked his way down to her waist, she was purring like a Bengal pussycat and black and blue be damned!

Show me a man who can give a great massage, and I'll show you a man who lives with a satisfied woman. Hell! Such a man could live with a satisfied harem! And it doesn't take a diploma from a school of Swedish massage. It only calls for care and concern, and a deep desire to make her feel so very very good, like the afterglow of orgasm on a bed of orchids floating on a perfumed pool.

First, have her lie on her tummy, arms down to the side (but not pressed against her sides). If she puts her arms over her head, it tightens the muscles across her shoulders. You can sit beside her or you can kneel astraddle her. (I like the latter, especially when he is also in the nude.) You can give a dry massage, without any lubrication, powder, alcohol, or etc., or you can use something. If you want to give her the ultimate in luscious feelings, I'd try a body oil. If you scan a women's magazine, you'll see why. We feline females have a big thing for lotions. Only one thing can feel better than a very suggestive application of lotion to all our skin surface, which, of course, means every square millimeter of skin. If you have a swollen bankroll, you can invest in some of those aromatic lotions and body oils. They don't necessarily *feel* any different from vegetable oil; but they smell more erotic. And that can be important too. If you're interested in saving a few coins to buy a bottle of wine for the bedroom, you might try safflower oil. If you want to add a fragrance, you can select one from a variety of essences at one of the stores catering to the psychedelic crowd. A few drops of appropriate essence, and you have everything you can get in the expensive *Brand X*.

I don't have any training in massage, but I can sure tell you what feels good. Translating the words into actions may be something else again. Anyway, I'll try.

Start across her shoulders. Muscles flow from her neck down and out to her shoulders. When she is relaxed, with her arms to her sides, you can feel the muscles in a relaxed state. That's the way you want it.

You can't massage a tense muscle. It hurts. If she is really uptight, all you can do is encourage her to relax. When she loosens up, start the massage. Begin with a rolling action of your fingers, your thumbs on either side of her spine and your other fingers kneading the shoulder muscles. "Easy does it," is the word. Keep in mind: you have two objectives: Make her feel all loose and languid; and turn her on. You may have had a massage and rubdown from some highly trained muscle man at the athletic club. And it really helped you unwind, didn't it? But that isn't the effect you're after when you put your hands on her.

Take care of her shoulders and upper arms, then move down her back. Let your fingertips work a soothing relaxation into each muscle along the way. Do you remember how they used to tell you how to place your hands in giving artificial respiration before the days of mouth-to-mouth? Well, that's something of the idea. Now keep your fingers in motion as you move down to her waist and the small of her back. If you give her the gift of massage, don't skimp. Make it total. Talk to her with your fingers—all over. Her buttocks, thighs, calves. The soles of her feet. Then have her roll over. From head to toe, make her feel like a satin rag doll.

Now, back to our topic of *twoplay*—

You've probably heard the story of the queen who was suffering from all sorts of vague ailments (probably very much like housewife's syndrome). The royal physician examined Her Royal Highness and handed down his learned diagnosis and prescription. Her Royal Highness, he said, needed more titillation of her clitoris. A doctor with a lot of moxie, I would say.

I have no intention of getting into that silly argument of is there more than one kind of female orgasm, clitoral, vaginal, or whatever. All I know is what feels good. I'll leave the technical specifications to someone else.

Before I say anything about how to stimulate her between the waist and the knees, please let me bore you with a word or two about this female anatomy of ours. I dislike lengthy discussions of what is located where, what it does, and what can be done with it. Since you are male, not female, however, you know more about your anatomy than ours. And it seems that your anatomy is much more obvious than a girl's. I've talked with a lot of gals with the same complaint: their men don't know exactly how or where to stimulate them. Maybe you do, but for the sake of such gals, let me conduct a quick guided tour:

That clitoris of hers isn't the easiest thing in the world to locate. It's more prominent in sex books than it is under her panties. It's the most sensitive spot on our female body, but it is small, and rather illusive. We want you to do nice things to it, but for some crazy reason we usually don't help you much. And we should. It's probably that old passive role we've been taught that keeps us from it. Even though it might keep us frustrated.

When a gal masturbates, nine out of ten times she will do so by stimulating her clitoris. So one thing is certain: she knows where it is and what to do to stimulate it. So if she wants you to pleasure her, and why wouldn't she, the obvious step would be for her to teach you how, to provide a clear, explicit, demonstration. With your encouragement, she probably will. But just in case she has hang-ups about such explicitness, you can still discover it for yourself.

The clitoris is just about right on the midline. You probably already know that. But *where* along that

line? About where a penis is located on a man: In
front. In other words, if she were lying flat on her
back with her legs squeezed tightly together, you could
probably still place your fingers on her clitoris. In my
very informal research (chats over a second cup of
coffee), I find a number of gals who complain that
their men, although willing and eager to pleasure and
arouse them, consistently head for the wrong place.
They start with a finger in the vagina. Or they stimulate the area very near the opening to the vagina, figuring, I guess, that the clitoris is somewhere around
there (and they miss by a very important inch, more
or less). I'm not saying your finger in her vagina
doesn't feel good. Sure it does, regardless of what
some male physiologists have said about all feeling
being in the clitoris (it isn't!). But most women go to
the clitoris first when they do it alone, and they like it
that way from their men. You can wander around later.

As to how to stimulate her? The same way she stim-
ulates herself. If she'll show you, great. If she won't,
well, you'll just have to try some of the more "popular" techniques and hope it throws the right switches.
Place your hand flat over her pubic area. Press it firmly and rotate your hand, making circles like polishing
a six-inch spot on a table top. Just be careful not to
pull hair. It hurts! Your fingers don't touch her clitoris directly this way, but it moves the lips on either
side back and forth along it in a most effective way.
(When we were little girls, we slid down banisters.
Same thing.)

She may prefer a more direct approach. Fine. Keep
your hand where it is, flat, with your fingers pointed
toward her feet. Then slip one finger between the lips.
Keep the finger extended and roll it from side to side.
You will probably be able to feel a little ridge running

lengthwise under your finger. That's the shaft of her clitoris. (It has a tiny shaft and a head just like your penis, but without an opening in the head.) When most gals masturbate, they don't stimulate the head of the clitoris directly too much. It's too sensitive to take much. Instead, they rub up and down along the side of the shaft, sometimes along both sides sort of like the way you masturbate. Try it. But a word of caution: That's an easily irritated area, especially if it isn't richly lubricated. You may think she will supply enough lubrication herself if she is sufficiently aroused. Well, ordinarily she will, but it won't necessarily reach her clitoris. The lubrication comes from the walls of the vagina, and if she is lying on her back, well, it isn't going to run uphill. You can "borrow" some from her vagina with your fingers. You can lubricate with saliva, but it dries fast. Or you can use some of that body lotion you employ in giving her a massage.

How long do you pleasure her clitoris? That depends on what you want and what she wants. But for selfish reasons and out of loyalty to my sex, I hope you will follow her desires. After all, you're trying to pleasure *her*. Hopefully, it's fun for you, but the emphasis is on giving her the goodies right then. If she's fair, she will reciprocate in turn. Be patient, and concentrate on her responses. She may want you to bring her to a climax with your fingers. Some of the time she probably will, but there may be times when she will want to hold back and climax when you do. Which, incidentally, is something I think men may have trouble understanding. Since you can ordinarily only make it once in an hour or so of love-making, the possibility of multiple orgasm may seem like a really great bonus, and why not take full advantage of it? Well, it is fun. But a gal doesn't always want it. Quality, in any case, is more important than quantity. If she does want to reach orgasm, you'll know it. She simply won't do or say anything to stop what you are doing for her.

Once she reaches her climax, you don't necessarily have to stop what you are doing. She can probably reach orgasm again—*if* that is what she desires. But give her a break before you go on. Make love to her in other ways during the breather before you return to it.

Another thing about her climax. Some men may call a halt to pleasuring with their fingers prematurely out of a fear that if a woman climaxes that way, she will lose interest in going on. Some gals may have talked themselves into feeling that way. They ought to straighten out their thinking. It doesn't need to slow her down at all, or reduce the height of her response at the finale.

One other area that is very sensitive to erotic stimulation is at the opening of the vagina. Moving your fingers in circles with your fingertips just inside can provide her with a highly charged experience. Try it.

Whatever you can do to stimulate her with your fingers, you can do with your lips and tongue. And perhaps better. The tongue is, indeed, a very versatile organ. You can extend or retract it, move it from side to side, up and down, and in circles. And it is very sensitive to touch as well as taste. A truly remarkable organ, the tongue. And for most adults of both sexes, the tongue is a sexual organ.

Oral sex strikes me as being in the position opposite to what Will Rogers said about the weather: "Everybody talks about it, but nobody does anything about it." With oral sex, everybody does it, but nobody wants to talk about it. This is changing, just as most attitudes about sex seem to be changing, but oral sex is still one of those things which bothers some people, more women perhaps than men. So what do we do about it? We can do it and enjoy it without any hang-ups. We can do it and feel guilty or "sick." We can shun it as "unnecessary" to a full and fulfilling sex life. And it just may be. To each his own! Or her own!

Assuming they both do want to expand their sex relations via oral sex, there are a few things the men should know about technique. Hopefully, his woman will be willing to take instructions from him in what she can do for him in this game.

Since your tongue isn't nearly as rough as your fingers (unless you're a cat), you can continue stimulating her with your tongue for a longer period of time and, most of the time, to a higher degree of intensity than you can with your fingers. And lubrication is never a problem. The first decision to be made is whether you are going to "serve" her, without any simultaneous "service" provided by her, or whether you want mutual oral sex. Let's take a how-to-do-it look at positions and techniques for the former first. You've decided to serve and increase her sexual desires. Several positions can be employed. If she isn't going to participate actively for the time, however, she should be encouraged to "relax and enjoy it." Just for the sake of pure feminine pleasure, and that is what you want to give her, isn't it, why not urge her to assume a position which will allow her to relax all over, like when you give her a massage, while you "take over the pleasuring." She might lie on her back, thighs apart, legs extended or knees flexed. You can either lie facing in the opposite direction as you would if she were going to make it mutual, or you can lie between her legs, extended in the same direction. In the former, you have to lie with your shoulders and upper body at least partly on top of her. The position has one big advan-

tage for a girl (and for you too): she has something of
yours to play with. But we were talking about having
her remain completely passive and relaxed to begin
with, weren't we? And in that case, this reversed position doesn't give you the best advantage. You have to
bring your head and chin down in order to reach what
you're interested in, which, I suppose, could give you
a crick in the neck. And you may not find the parts of
her body you seek as accessible. Stretched out lengthwise between her thighs may be mechanically preferable, but if the two of you are in bed, you may have to
extend, with legs dangling, over the foot of the bed.
It's a position which works fine, however, on the floor
before the fireplace.

You can also have her place her legs over your
shoulders while she lies on her back and you kneel up-
right between her thighs. You'll have to place your
arms beneath her back and buttocks in that position or
she may quickly develop an aching back unless she is
the sort of gal who does thirty sit-ups before breakfast
every day. Other than that, the position has a lot to offer, which makes it worth trying. You can have her sit
on the edge of a chair while you kneel or sit before her,
but that is less of a "totally relaxed" position. It might
be better if you had her lie back across the bed (or a
table) with her feet on the floor. In any case, do try a
few variations. There is never one consistently "best"
way when it comes to the art of love-making.

Positions for mutual oral love are more limited. No
matter how you go about it, it comes down simply to
reversing your positions—head to toe. You can lie
above her; she can lie above you; or you can lie "facing" each other on your sides. And that's it. The one
on top can be on hands and knees or lying prone. It's

your preference, and hers, but a gentleman lover always considers the desires of his mistress.

When you are stimulating her clitoris with your mouth and tongue, you can use both hands to part her lips (labia). When they are widely parted (but gently, please), the clitoris is a little bit more exposed, all the better to get to. Since you can move your tongue in any direction, use some variety. A rapid flicking of just the tip of your tongue is positively delightful. But then so is a slow extended licking (think of a double-decker ice cream cone that you want to keep from melting in the summer sun). And don't overlook the possibilities you can offer her with your lips. Think of the clitoris as a tiny nipple. It can be sucked the same way you do with her breasts. You might try drawing it between your lips and doing nice things to it with the tips of your tongue. If you keep that up for more than fifteen seconds and she doesn't "come," take her pulse and check her breathing; she may be dead! Some men never try any vaginal stimulation with their tongue. I don't know why. Maybe they mentally compare the tongue with the penis and feel that because the tongue isn't as big or as long or whatever as the penis, they can't give much to her vagina with the tongue. They're wrong. Remember those things I said about how to kiss a girl? Well think of it this way: she has a second set of lips, and another mouth just as eager to be kissed and loved with your tongue. If she straddles your face while you lie on your back, you can kiss her into a marvelous state of loving response.

One more suggestion for twoplay: A hand vibrator is an appliance no lovers' bedroom should be without. The ones that fit on the back of the hand, the kind barbers use in giving a scalp massage, are great. You can slip it on when you give her a massage (and she can use it when she massages you). And the vibrator on the back of your hand when you place your fingers on her clitoris is a sensory experience which must be felt to be appreciated. You've probably seen ads for those "personal" vibrators, the sort which are shaped like a phallus and designed to stimulate the same place your imagination would tell you. They are battery operated and do have something to offer. It depends on the gal's preferences. Personally, the hard plastic feel of those vibrators leaves me less than totally turned on. Maybe the manufacturers should hire a woman engineer to tackle a redesigning.

In addition to the nice things you can do for her with a vibrator (and some equally nice things she can do to you), there is another very practical reason for investing in a vibrator. The more a gal works at developing her sensual responsiveness, the more she will find herself capable of feeling all she would like to feel, and responding in all the ways both of you desire. Raised in this uptight female world of ours, we have to learn to start our feminine motors and keep them running. If a gal doesn't learn to do it, and do it well, for herself, no man will have much luck doing it for her. She can use that vibrator "practicing" sensual lessons following her afternoon bath. I don't care *what* somebody else might think she's doing. I say she's practicing her lessons in turning on. I could go on for another chapter on those lessons, but this isn't a book for mistresses; it's one for lovers.

CHAPTER SEVEN

The How of It: Into Orbit

I don't care what they say about variations in love-making, and a lot of good things can be said about them, there is something about that first long, deep thrust of a penis into her vagina that is absolutely incomparable for a woman. It makes her feel she's all woman, and that being a woman is a very good thing. Some men may prefer going "all the way" by other means, by oral sex, for example, but I think if given the choice, most gals would vote for reaching the finale in the delightfully basic way: her man's organ buried to the hilt.

So why is it so many gals claim they are left high and dry after what their men hope will leave them limp and loving? If they like the way God made little boys so much, why do they complain so much about what big boys do with what God gave them?

I can't say for sure. I'll admit I even have difficulty

relating to many such gals. I freely confess to a bias (you might even call it an obsession) in favor of what the Freudian shrinks call "phallic worship." But I can at least repeat what I've heard from many frustrated wives.

The number-one complaint: "He's all through before I reach my climax." Which may mean (1) she has a low appetite for sex, (2) he has trouble with control, or (3) they started the finale before they should have. I'll save (1) and (2) for the next chapter. Let's talk about (3).

The one obvious answer to the question, "When should the couple begin the final act: coitus?" is: "When they are both ready." Does that answer help anyone? Not much, unless you stop to think of something else which is rather obvious: You just about never hear the complaint from a man. Oh, I'm not saying men are walking around in a state of perpetual "readiness." That may be an accusation by some women (and the dream of some!) but we know it isn't so. What I am saying is that once a man is aroused, he can go all the way at any time and reach his climax except in those circumstances where he loses his erection. He doesn't have to go through a prolonged period of stimulation. All the preliminary love-making should be as much fun for a man as for a woman, but it isn't "necessary" to him once he has an erection. So what we are talking about is how soon *she* is sufficiently aroused to be able to go all the way to orgasm when he enters her. It sounds selfish when I say it, but the answer to the question "When?" is "When *she* is ready."

That drops it squarely in her lap. If she gives the go-ahead when she isn't ready, she has no one to blame but herself. If her lover goes ahead without finding out if she is ready, he is the bad guy. There is nothing which beats good communication where sex is concerned. You can't read her mind, and she can't read yours. Furthermore, there is one bit of misinformation which should be laid to rest in some deep pit: Every man man knows a woman secretes a lubricating fluid when she becomes aroused, and some men have the idea that wetness between her thighs means a gal is fully ready. It doesn't. All it means is that she is aroused. But she isn't a man. Arousal, for a woman, is not an "all or none" condition. There are degrees of arousal, and she may be aroused in increasing degrees over quite a period of twoplay before she is at a high enough pitch to ensure a climax when they culminate the action.

How she goes about communicating her desires and feelings state could open up a whole discussion in itself. For all the wrong reasons (and can there be any *right* reasons?) couples don't talk about sex. Or they don't talk about it enough. Or they don't talk about the right things in sex. If she is reluctant to discuss all those nitty-gritty matters, you will have to bring out all those male persuasions of yours to get her to open up. If you also refuse to talk about it, throw in the towel and take up crossword puzzles for excitement. What communication does go on in sex is all too often as clear as a mud puddle at midnight. We try to send too many messages on a non-verbal level. She shoves your hand away, or moves sideways, or lifts up a little, or pushes down, and you are supposed to know what she's saying. All I can say is, "Good luck!" Unless you know her every bit as well as she knows herself, you are going to miss a high percentage of the time. But I'm not going to blame it all on her poorly developed communication skills. You have a responsibility in it also. If you ignore those not so subtle signs she is giving you, she can't help herself or you even if she draws pictures or shouts. She's facing a delicate matter in this. She wants you to be the lord and master, especially in bed. She doesn't want to seem critical. She doesn't want to bruise your ego. And she sure doesn't want to give the impression she thinks you don't make it as a lover. She's walking a tightwire. She wants to keep the messages as subtle as possible, and probably as non-verbal as possible. Then, if her lover picks up the messages and interprets them correctly, it says something very special to her: he is lovingly aware of *her*. She doesn't want to rule the bedroom as director and teacher. But she is faced with the problem of how to get the message of her desires across without appearing to take over.

Encourage her to tell you what things are especially appealing to her. The conversation doesn't have to take place during the love-making. Sure, she can say this or that feels good. These responses are part of the love-making. But conversations over what each of you finds sexually exciting can be held at other times, and they should be. Not only are such conversations informative, they're fun. Still, you can learn a lot about her responses by concentrating on her. And you can score higher in the sex games if you encourage her to become an active and equally responsible participant.

The go-ahead signal is left to her. Ordinarily, she can do herself the most good toward ensuring her peak orgasm if she waits until she is right on the brink of reaching it before she takes your penis and guides it into her vagina. If she does, then the first few thrusts should be sufficient to trigger her explosion. To try to raise her passions from lukewarm to boiling *after* you enter her is usually a futile attempt. Most men are not going to hold off that long. And if that happens, you're going to feel they flubbed as a lover. You may not have. She may have taken things in hand too soon.

She can sometimes help bring herself close to the brink just before guiding you in if she takes your organ in her hand and rubs the head of it rapidly on her clitoris in the way she might do with her own finger. She should know, after all, the speed, pressure, etc., which feels best to her if she has been practicing her afternoon exercises. And beyond the fact that it turns her on to put her hand around it, the head of your penis has a smooth texture which feels especially good for such self-stimulation. At that point, you usually even supply some lubrication of your own. Watch out, however. If you let her go on too long, you may finish sooner than you plan and not where you hoped, thus defeating her purpose and yours.

I said that first long, deep, thrust of a penis into her vagina is absolutely incomparable for a woman. Let me expand on that a bit and sing its praises on behalf of womanhood. I'm not sure what it means psychologically to a woman, but it seems to me that it carries with it a "taking of his woman" on the man's part and a surrender to his manhood on her part. The whole sexual scenario between man and woman has an element of mock combat to it. The man conquers the woman and she surrenders. He scores a conquest. He takes her, throws her to the ground, and thrusts his sexual organ into hers. It is when she "accepts the inevitable" that she finds the satisfaction in her "vanquishment" for which she has been waiting with increasing eagerness. Don't rob her of it. Let her enjoy it to the fullest. You don't have to become "active" as soon as you enter. You can penetrate fully all the way, and stay there, motionless, while she absorbs the indescribable feeling of fullness you provide. It may be tempting to you to begin thrusting in and out right away, and she knows that, but it won't cripple you, will it, to hold off for a moment of timelessness, a short period of time in which to revel in a physical union which tells her she is part of you and you are part of her.

While you hold that position, totally joined in the closest and most meaningful embrace possible to a man and woman, you can express your love for her in a variety of ways, position permitting. Tell her how good it feels to you. Express your love for her; a girl never tires of that. If you are face to face, why not continue the kisses? Run your hands, lightly, caressingly, over her skin—her shoulders, arms, sides. Take time. How should you better spend it than in a total experience of touching?

If your goal is to love her and be loved in return, that female psychology of hers should be kept in a place of importance. I read somewhere a psychoanalyst's views of what goes on unconsciously in lovemaking. He said penetration is, for a man, a desire to return to the womb; for the woman, it is a desire to have him become the child in her womb. That's a little much for me, but I can agree that it has some pretty deep and complicated meanings for my own sex. The key, I think, is that a woman doesn't want sex to be something which is done *to* her, or *for* her, or even something she *does* for a man. She wants it to be a shared *experience*. The word "oneness" has a special meaning and importance to her. The biblical description "two shall become one" says a lot to a woman. I'm not sure it says as much to a man. I don't want to contribute more to the mystique and mystery which has been built around womanhood, but I can't, on the other hand, escape the conclusion that there is something kind of mysterious about our female psychology which puzzles us probably as much as it baffles men. Maybe I won't help clear up the mystery in what I have to say. I may just confuse matters more. But for whatever it's worth, here are the impressions of one woman: First, men and women are not only different, they are more different than a lot of the modern intellectuals and female militants would have us believe. When it comes to sex, those differences show themselves in very bold relief. Understanding them can turn what might otherwise be a less than fully satisfying *act* into an experience which transforms, enhances, unifies, and just generally makes worthwhile every facet of one's life—at least for a woman.

There have been a lot of words written about these differences (in addition to all those written denying them). I think most of them talk about supposed differences which, at least to a woman, are pretty much "So what?" Who really cares whether women think more intuitively and men more logically so long as they can live and love together? And does it really help you or me to decide women are more "emotional" than men? I *am* a woman, and that no doubt means a lot of things. It means I'm similar to all other women in many respects and probably different in many, but most important, it means I am *not* a man. I don't think like a man, feel like a man, or, in many respects, act like a man. And I wouldn't want to. Any gal who envies a man his world has never made it as a woman. If I'm going to live with a man, however, I think I have to try hard to understand his world and how and why he acts and reacts the way he does. And if a man wants to be loved by a woman, I think he has to work at trying to understand this admittedly confusing way we gals function and feel.

It may be too black and white to describe it this way, but it seems to me that a man looks at sex as an act he engages in with his woman. She approaches it seeking a state of being, a relationship, a fusion of their two separate personalities. Maybe there *is* something maternal in it since a woman physically takes him into her body and psychologically encloses him within her. She wants to be "possessed" by him while she, at the same time, engulfs him. I suppose if somehow a woman could totally and continually enclose her man within her body, life for her would be a never ending orgasm. (Now if that isn't mystical enough for you, I don't know what might be.) Women talk a lot today about their need for "fulfillment." Men, on the other hand, are more apt to talk about achievement. I don't care what some gals may *think* they mean by fulfillment. They can rattle on all they like about seeking fulfillment through pursuits running all the way from the PTA presidency to a career as a major league umpire, but I'll stand squarely on the conviction that no woman, and I do mean *no* woman, reaches that never-never land of bliss called "fulfillment" unless it is with and through a man—*her* man. In a few words: *A Woman Becomes a Woman Only Through a Man.* She needs her man to affirm her womanhood, to tell her repeatedly in every way that he sees her as a woman, a desirable woman, *his* woman. It can't be done just in bed—ever. It must be injected into all phases and facets of their relationship. If it is lacking at other times, it won't be made up for in bed. The frustration at not being affirmed as a woman is what lies beneath the all too common female complaint: "I don't feel he loves me; he just uses me."

In the sex experience, you affirm her womanhood by showing your awareness of her—and your own *presence.* What I mean by your presence does not, obviously, have anything to do with your physical presence. Of course you're there. You can't have sex by long distance. I mean *presence* which shows her your thoughts are directed toward her, that your mind hasn't gone off someplace else. Maybe they don't intend to do so, but it seems a lot of men are guilty of this mental turn-off during love-making. They make a gal feel as if she no longer exists for them as soon as they penetrate the objective. All other gestures of love pretty well come to a halt: kissing, caressing, words of love (including those arousing four-letter words). And when they do, she may end up feeling even further away from her man rather than closer.

I see man-woman love-making as composed of feelings, actions, and that very hard to define thing we call a "relationship." If any one of the three is missing, the whole business is bound to fall flat—at least for my sex. Without physical feelings, which are pleasurable, what point would there be in sex, and if either partner has trouble enjoying the feelings he should be enjoying, no one has to be told how much everything else between them can begin to fall apart. Without actions and movements, you might be good for a yoga meditation, but in the sack you'll be good only for sleeping. That hard-to-define one, the "relationship," is the one I want to promote, and I mean really *push,* on behalf of women. Don't get me wrong. I have no desire to take anything away from the physical—either feelings or actions. Perish the thought! But all three should be kept present when the couple come together in love-making, and men, I'm sorry to say, often become kind of totally absorbed in the actions and movements (and maybe just their own feelings) and forget the relationship and the gal until it's all over. Then they want to know if she reached a climax. Are they really concerned or just on a male ego trip?

Even your movements after you enter her have a lot to do with maintaining and enhancing the *relationship*. If we get a bit "anatomical" for a minute, maybe I can clarify what I mean by that. When she guides your penis into her, she feels that penetration and the sensation of fullness through every last fiber of her body. For a woman, it's as if a part of her has been missing, an important part, and she has been at least vaguely aware of the void it left. Now it is returned: she is whole again. That's why it is particularly pleasurable to a gal when her man enters her all the way and gives her time to enjoy being filled with him to the fullest extent before continuing with further movements which at least partly mean a withdrawal from her. You might even, if you are looking for a "total experience" for your gal, try this one: In a prone position facing each other (either you on top, her on top, or on your sides) have her guide you in. Make it slow, very slow, until you are in all the way and pressed tightly against each other. Then, holding her and caressing her lovingly, *talk*. Yes, I did say talk. Without moving in and out, just staying fully within her body, share your thoughts. It's an absolutely fabulous time for reminiscing over days and nights of loving, fantasies, and desires. You can stay aroused while at the same time being relaxed, a condition which might seem almost impossible. The greatest advantage, however, is psychological: it offers an almost overwhelming feeling of oneness, just about everything your woman wants the relationship to be.

When you do get around to starting your movements, they can also become a true art form. Honestly! And you don't have to be a ballet dancer either.

Here we have another of those many differences between the sexes. A man gets his greatest stimulation from those long strokes in and out. That's fine, but it can create problems for a gal. There are few men who have much in the way of staying power with thrusting movements. Don't get me wrong; I'm not saying don't do any plunging and thrusting. But unless you have far above average control, and don't feel you're a loser if you don't, hold off on it until you—*and your gal*—are ready to go for the final climax. She also enjoys the plunging strokes, especially for the finale, but there are other movements which give her deep, deep satisfaction, movements which can prolong your love-making (and isn't that a worthy goal?). For one thing, you can, while fully penetrating her, move your body up and down over her (if you are face-to-face over her, this means moving your shoulders above hers, up and down, without moving your pelvis; if you have a wall or bed footboard to press your feet against, movement can be increased by "rising and lowering" on the balls of your feet). Think about it for a minute: She is benefiting from great movement of your penis inside her, but without you having to engage in those thrusting movements. I think the reason most men avoid this, or maybe just never try it, is that they know what turns them on the most and they just naturally figure a woman will only be turned on by the same actions. Another variation is a rotary movement. Keep all the way in, but move your pelvis in a rotary, twisting, movement. It's more than slightly fantastic, and the closer you're pressed against her, the better.

Some of those sex books you may have read might have stressed the importance of manually stimulating her clitoris during coitis. Some of them make it sound as if that penis of yours in her vagina is never enough, that a gal can't reach orgasm in any way other than by direct titillation of the clitoris, and they give, as "proof," all sorts of scientific evidence of a lack of nerve endings in the vagina or something. Well, maybe a lot of us gals are like the bumblebee. The aeronautical engineers can prove the bumblebee isn't constructed in a way which makes flying possible. But the bumblebee, not knowing this, goes on flying. I don't know anything about those nerve endings, but I know there are more ways to reach orgasm than just one. How do the experts explain it? They've tried saying that the penis in the vagina is indirectly stimulating the clitoris. O.K., but what about the gals who can reach orgasm by stimulation of their nipples or by anal intercourse? Phooey to such experts' opinions.

I'm not saying, however, that your fingers on her clitoris while you are inside her doesn't add something extra. She may enjoy it that way, and with some gals it may be necessary. With others, it may be only an added bonus. And there are a number of women who enjoy it sometimes, but not always, or they may enjoy it at the beginning, just after he enters, but want only the feel of his penis as they approach climax. The same might be said of another popular form of added stimulation: anal stimulation with the finger. We gals are variable in our desires and responses from one time to the next. The winning lover makes it a point to try to discover what things will turn her on the most each time they make love.

Added stimulation by your fingers will obviously be easier to manage in some positions than in others. Which brings up the question of variations in position. This is something I've always felt was worked to death in the paperback sex manuals. I think some of those authors have the idea they can win a prize if they can come up with one more position than their rivals. Some even number them. ("Which do you think you'd like, honey, number thirty-four or number seventeen?") It all seems pretty ridiculous. In the first place, unless you're a contortionist, there are only so many things you can do with your body and hers. There are ways they just won't bend. There are only three basic ways of doing it: face-to-face, approaching her from behind, and with her astride, facing you or away from you. All those minor variations which they list as different positions are ordinarily what any couple would discover moving around and finding new delights together. Sex can be accomplished standing, kneeling, sitting, and lying. It seems to me that couples who are either too inhibited or too lacking in imagination to try out variations in their love-making are not going to be helped by all those numbered acrobatics, not even if a feature-length movie is included with the purchase of the book. Sooo—I'm not going to bore you with tedious descriptions of positions, and I'm not including photos. But let me make a strong pitch for experimentation in positions. It offers a couple of plusses: For one, when you shift positions you enter her from a different angle. That penis of yours presses against different spots, all of them good; why neglect them? With her astride, for example, you can penetrate deeper than you would in a prone position, and tonight that may be the feeling she wants, at least during part of the scenario of loving. Insertion from behind is a very different experience, for a woman perhaps more so than for a man. It may be her preference. You'll never know unless you try it. The other plus offered by variations is psychological. It breaks up the routine and helps keep that wolf of boredom away from the bedroom door.

I don't think Dr. Kinsey and the other poll takers ever got around to asking women to name their favorite positions. Or men either for that matter. If they had, my guess is that all those scores of positions are of much more interest to the how-to-do-it writers than they are to the average gal. From my own informal random sample, two positions seem to win feminine popularity: the woman astride, and the "conventional" position with the man on top. The astride position gives her a chance to exercise some control of the action, and this reversal of roles is a pleasant change. It also allows her to "serve" him; she does the "work" while he lies back and enjoys it. The face-to-face position with him on top is, I would bet, still the favorite of most gals, not because they are uptight conservatives, but because it provides more total touching than any other and a lot of opportunity to be loved by his hands and lips. In case I haven't made the point clear enough: We gals do love to be loved. Not just laid, my male friend, *loved*. Anyway, try out your variations, but pay some loving attention to her responses and what she may like to start with, finish with, and play with in between.

In reading over the last dozen pages or so, I notice I've several times said something about the "finale" in a way which implies that the orgasm is the conclusion of the love-making. Well, scratch all that. That mutual climax should be the high point, but *not* the ending. Your male sex interest may drop like a lead tennis ball as soon as you come off and you're ready for sleepy time, but a girl isn't built that way. Her passions cool down about as slowly as they build up. She wants to float down in a parachute (or maybe a slowly descending balloon), not be dropped, kerboom, from the heights. The one who first suggested withdrawal as a

means of birth control must have hated women. Even
Freud, who some feel was not the truest friend women
ever had, thought *that* practice was *sick!* You don't
have to withdraw two seconds after you climax. If you
are lying on top and you're pretty heavy, you might
shift your weight a little to one side, but you don't
have to take it out. Stay where you are and love her
with words, kisses, and tenderness. If you suddenly remember an important phone call you have to make at
that time, all I can say is, "Try raising guppies; you'll
never make it as a lover!" One of the all-time experiences of closeness comes when you fall slowly in each
other's arms without withdrawing. True bliss—feminine version—can't be far from that. Let me say a
word, however, about the minority of gals who jump
out of bed like electrified frogs to run to the bathroom
as soon as the final plunge is over. Either by faulty
training ("Tales my mother never should have told me
—but did") or by some silly attitudes toward sex
("It's so messy!"), such gals have this thing about
douching right after. Maybe it's a rejection of men
(Do women's libbers douche right after sex when, as,
and if they have sex—with men, that is?). Anyway, if
that is her thing, you have an educational job on your
hands. Maybe you can threaten to poke holes in her
douche bag. Douching is for the next morning and
with the evening bath *before*, not *after*. If you are the
one who jumps up and washes off, I don't know what
to say except you leave something to be desired as
both a gentleman and as a lover. It's a lousy put-down
of your mistress, kind of like using a mouthwash after
you kiss her.

A final word for considerate lovers: Don't let the
night before be forgotten by the next morning. It isn't
a passing event to her, and she doesn't like to think it's

that casual to you. Try telling her, over your morning coffee, how good it was. Why not thank her for the pleasures she provided. You would thank her, wouldn't you, if she served your favorite meal? Well doesn't good sex do as much for you? If it doesn't, you must have a godawful weight problem.

Now, since none of us can hope to bat 1.000 in the games of love, shall we take a look at errors in loving and what can be done about them? And take heart; a lot can.

CHAPTER EIGHT

Three Strikes
Isn't the Ball Game

If you are the perfect lover, I can't help you. Nobody can. You're doomed to a lonely life. What girl could tolerate living with the perfect lover? It would drive any ordinary, human female up a slippery elm. The inadequacy feelings she would suffer would force her to bury her head in a sand pile. Hopefully, your mistress doesn't have a perfect lover. She has a *man*. He's fallible. Sometimes difficult. And he sometimes strikes out.

And what do I mean by a strike-out? Maybe not what you think. What I'm talking about are those times when the usually smooth-running relationship runs onto a bump. I'm not talking about a major breakdown between the two of you. If it reaches that point, you may have to decide either to seek some professional help or accept a parting of the ways.

The strike-out might occur in any of a number of

ball parks. It might be in communication. You let go with a "casual" comment (defined as one with poor connections between brain and tongue), and she reacts with typical feminine emotion. (If a man gets emotional in the same way, he's considered less than a man; if we do it, well, we are, after all, women.) It may be only an instant flare-up, forgotten a minute later. On the other hand, words may fly back and forth and the rest of the day may be a deep freeze for you. It's a genuine strike-out, but it isn't the whole ball game. The key to building and maintaining the good thing you want happening between the two of you lies in keeping the strike-outs at a minimum and bouncing back as quickly as possible after that third strike.

I'm not going to try to go into all the ways we can goof things up in living with someone we love. I couldn't even begin to count them all, and I'm sure there are quite a few I haven't even thought of—but somebody has. I do want to talk about a few things of importance to men, important because they involve those hard-to-figure-out differences between you males and us females.

At the top of the list, as if you had to be told, are those emotions. I guess we all want to believe we are sensible, calm, rational, and all those other adjectives that mean we are grown-up. But let's face it, we aren't. At least not all the time. And is there a man walking about who has not at some time despaired of ever coping with the irrationality of his woman? Well, I'm not going to say the members of my sex behave in very rational ways. Much of the time we don't. But I'm not sure our averages are worse than our mates'. My own theory is that both males and females are about equally rational or irrational, but in different ways. And in trying to spell out how I think they're different, I'm going to get in trouble with the women's libbers again (yet? still?).

Women are more emotional; men are more logical. Now there's a quaint old idea. It stacks up alongside the folklore that blacks have natural rhythm and redheads are hot-tempered. And I think it's just about as true, meaning it *isn't*. But, before we brand it as a male chauvinist lie and a putdown of my newly liberated sex, I think we can dig around in to see if there isn't a grain or two of truth buried there.

I believe there is. But I don't think it makes the male approach more rational—or vice versa. Males have been brainwashed into believing that any show of emotion (other than anger) is, for men and boys, a no-no. So you shove them down in your head, develop ulcers and coronaries, and play it cool. We gals are encouraged to let it all hang out, and can any man doubt that we do? Men take a good logical two plus two approach, which may, admittedly, be a pretty good one. But if the guy comes up with an answer of five, then the approach isn't much help. It might be as well if he used a roulette wheel for his decision-making. Women, at least some of us, arrive at decisions right out of the blue by bolt of lightning intuition. It may strike you as pretty farfetched, but if we have a good batting average of right answers, why should anyone care if we get them from a Ouija board?

Doesn't it really come down to whether or not one male and one female can talk to one another and have something we call communication come out of it? Strike-outs may not all be in communication, but communication is the number-one way to bounce back. You can shovel a little sand over the mess, ignore it, wait a couple of days for it to blow over, and maybe in time things will get back to normal and the ice will thaw. But wow! Isn't life short enough? Why blow part of it losing hours that way? Why not use those verbal skills of yours and bring it all out where the two of you can come to grips with it?

Why not indeed? And who would disagree? But that's the rub. Communication isn't just something you decide to do and then set out and do it. In the first place, even if you want to, she has to be willing to also, and I'm sorry to say a lot of my fellow females run away from communication attempts with that sensitive little-girl nonsense of "I'm just too hurt to talk." Or they dash off to the bathroom and lock the door. (Advice: Learn to pick locks.) In the second place, you can talk at each other for hours and never make it as far as communication goes. You might just wind up in a *Virginia Woolf* verbal blood bath and make things worse than they were to start.

I'm not going to go into a long thing here on how to talk to that gal of yours or get her to talk to you and get something from it. That would make a book in itself. I'll just give a few techniques that have been tested and found to work.

Do you ever play tennis? Well, even if you don't, I'm sure you know as much about it as I do, which isn't much, and for the type of tennis match I'm going to talk about, you don't have to know too much about the game. This is a technique for communication. It's pretty hokey maybe and it doesn't permit those free-swinging words couples throw back and forth at each other, but if it gets you closer to that loving closeness you want, it may be worth trying.

The "tennis court" is wherever the two of you choose to do your talking. It could be a bedroom, living room, or parked car. The car is great—no interruptions. Select the tennis court with care. You can't play an adequate game on a court cluttered up with obstacles. They get in the way and you break your neck falling over them. You can't communicate in a room cluttered up with other people around. If you have kids, send them out or wait until they're off to bed. And don't try communicating about anything important with friends present. Nobody, but nobody, communicates at a cocktail party. Turn off the TV. It can really get in your way. Just about the time you get close to conversational nitty-gritty, something comes flickering on the tube and you never get back to it.

The "tennis ball" is the topic under discussion. It should be kept as narrow and specific as possible. You can't go anywhere with a broad, general topic. If you say you want to talk about sex, you may run up against a dead end even if she agrees. It's just too broad. *What* about sex? If you suggest talking about why she always eats garlic before going to bed with you, it has been kept narrow enough to deal with (the conversation, not the garlic). Also, serve and return only a single ball. You can't play with a half dozen tennis balls flying back and forth at the same time. If you come at her with one of those compound problems, like, "I'd like to know why you spend so much money, just like your mother does, and yet bitch at me whenever I buy a six-pack of beer and never want to go all-out in bed," you have slammed a whole basket of balls across the net. Which one do you want her to play? She can't respond to all of them at once.

There are two big rules in the communication tennis match: (1) You must turn off the emotions; and (2) you can't walk out before the match is over. To that first one, just about everybody flips. "Shut off my emotions? Absurd! It can't be done. When she comes on with that bitchy put-down of hers, I can't just sit

there with a marshmallow-eating grin on my face and
take it. I blow my skull; it's just the way I am." To
which all I can say, lover, is— (I decided my editor
wouldn't let me say it after all.) I don't care what you
feel on a gut level; you don't have to spread it all over
the verbal landscape. You can turn it off and talk to
her with your cool intact. If you can't, don't blame her
if she enrolls you in nursery school or shoves a pacifier
in your mouth (with her fist). For the second one,
self-discipline (that old, worn-out, hyphenated imper-
ative) is demanded. It's tempting, when things get
rough and you start wondering if she is going to drag
out the big club she could use on your vulnerability, to
remember you had something else to do which was
more important than talking things out with her. You
dash off to the office, make a phone call, or run to the
john. Cop out! Cop out! Cop out! Stay and fight it
out (with yourself) like a man. If what you have to
talk about is important to the two of you and you
won't have time to finish it, hold off starting it until
later when you can carry it through. And once you
start, don't quit until you resolve whatever the issue
may be. O.K., so maybe it takes you all night. It's only
a little lost sleep, and that won't kill either of you.

When you play your communication tennis match-
es, try to listen to her. The idea is to try to understand
one another, not score points. Maybe, with your superior logic, you can prove her wrong, but where does it
get you? You're never going to see eye-to-eye on everything, but is it crucial to your ego to make an issue
out of each difference? She does have those female
feelings, you know. They may be hard to understand
unless you make a major effort to psyche her out.
And they may even be annoying. But remember, it's
those same emotions of hers that enable her to be sen-

sitive to your needs and give you all the things a woman can give a man. She can turn off the tears and temper as well as you can, but you won't help your cause by lecturing her about it. The idea, you'll recall, is to manipulate and seduce her into giving you what you want. And that means *love* her into it.

After you have talked out whatever went wrong, what then? There are some problems that are not resolved by an "I'm sorry" and a make-up kiss. They may call for a new plan of action. Figure out what you can do in the future to try to keep it from happening again—whatever the "it" might be. And don't get hung-up with the idea you might be giving in and giving in is a defeat to your he-manliness. "Giving" is serving your self-interest by serving hers and reaping the benefits and goodies she has for you.

There are some problems, however, that call for more than good communication and some firm resolves. You have to know what to do and what not to do, especially when it comes to strike-outs in sex. And that's what they are: strike-outs. There is no such thing as "sexual incompatibility." Some gals may turn you on; others may not. And sorry to say, you may not make sparks for every gal on the block. But that's just a fact of life and chemistry. It isn't some physical thing called "incompatibility," at least in all cases in which there isn't something physically wrong with either partner, and don't worry, you'd probably know it if you are or she is. So if it isn't physical, maybe something can be done about it. Let's take a look at *what.*

Premature ejaculation: This is one of those labels which seldom makes much sense. I've listened to many gals who complain their men come too soon or too fast. But too fast for whom? I'm sure a lot of guys get a bum rap when it comes to this business not because of their hang-up but because of a gal who couldn't make it with six relay lovers over eight hours. Before we blame it all on slow-responding females, however, let's admit that most men do, at least once in a while, have trouble holding back as long as they, and their women, might like. And there are some things which don't help much and some others which do.

One thing you can forget entirely is those deadening creams and salves which are supposed to make you less sensitive to stimulation. Who knows, maybe they do. I suppose you could also inject novocaine into the head of your penis, but what a miserable thought that is. What live gal would want to be "serviced" by a dead lover? Besides, everybody who has studied the "problem" has concluded that it isn't the result of too much sexual sensitivity (although it might be a consoling thought). If those salves worked and were the only things which did, it might do you more good to buy her one of those personal vibrators and find a way to satisfy yourself. Why not? You can't enjoy it without any feeling, can you?

Another suggestion you might just as well forget under most circumstances is more frequent sex. It doesn't help much. For one thing, coming too soon isn't often the result of going without it unless it has really been a long time with nothing at all (like maybe six months at sea). You could have sex at four in the afternoon and at eleven that evening still come too soon when you try for a repeat. Sure frequency may make some difference, but the big difference will be in whether you are able to perform the next time that soon after. One sex manual suggested masturbating an hour or two before going to bed with your gal. The author had to be kidding. Or maybe he was trying to show what a sexual superman he is. Just don't take it seriously. It isn't the answer.

That's what won't help. Now what will? Two or three things. First, there is a psychological business involved in this. It has to do with anxiety. If you're afraid you are going to "come" too fast, you probably will. In fact, if you are afraid of anything, including that gal of yours, you may lose your control. It can even become a kind of vicious cycle. You have one of those times when you can't hold off long enough. The next time you try to make it, that memory of the last time pops into your head: "What if it happens again?" There is an almost certain chance this will happen if your gal has pulled a dramatic frustration act the time before. You get uptight at the thought and, sure enough, it happens again and you feel wiped out. A few more times, and you have a habit stronger than nail-biting and black coffee.

If it has happened more than once or twice in the past and you have suffered some abrasions to your masculine ego, maybe it's time to take some of your thinking out for an airing, a real down-to-earth reexamination. Are you telling yourself a lot of doom words about the situation? Such as, "If I try, I may fail again; it will leave her climbing the wall and she'll think I'm not much of a man"? If that is your thinking, you're setting yourself up for a series of less than fun-filled experiences. And does that sort of defeatism make any sense? Of course not. It makes one part of sex the whole thing. Good grief! There's more to it than that. And there is a whale of a lot more to a man than the timing of a purely reflex reaction. To make a few seconds difference in timing a measure of success or failure has got to be some kind of craziness. So if you have developed any of that "I'm no damn good" thinking, get ruthless with yourself. Take out what's in your head and overhaul it.

If your gal is contributing to your negative thoughts, it calls for some work on the relationship and/or her response, not on sex techniques. The gal who acts out that "You left me high and dry" little-girl-frustrated bit is her own worst enemy. And somebody ought to tell her. No matter what some women think, every smart gal knows that the most important thing to a man in love-making is bringing his gal to a climax. And unless she is frigid (and he didn't make her that way), he can, regardless of how soon he "comes." There is, after all, more than one way for a gal to reach a climax. Several, in fact. It seems to me there may be a couple of reasons why a gal would be left without it (assuming she isn't frigid). For one thing, I know a number of women have the idea a man can go a lot longer than most men ordinarily can. If it takes her ten minutes after he enters before she reaches orgasm, she isn't going to find many men who could ever meet her "demands." If he reaches his climax in less than ten minutes, I suppose you could call it "premature." But premature to what? Not to what is normal, only to her. As I said in the last chapter, it should be up to her to signal when she is ready, and I mean *momentarily* ready. If she takes the responsibility and gives the go-ahead only when she is ready to climax momentarily, she isn't going to be frustrated by her own unrealistic expectancies. Another thing, I believe, is a lingering emphasis on "simultaneous" orgasm. Until just a few years ago, just about all the sex books made reaching orgasm at the same moment *the* key to sexual bliss. And in just about all erotic novels, the man and woman "dissolve" in a *mutual* explosion of sexual rockets. That nonsensical idea just may have sown more seeds of sexual misery than any other. It made sexual "success" a bit like spinning two roulette wheels at the same time and expecting them to come up with the same number. I'm not saying that simultaneous orgasm is impossible. Quite a few couples experience it just about every time, probably because the feeling of the man ejaculating triggers the gal's climax. The point is: it isn't essential to satisfaction for either partner. If it happens, fine. If it doesn't, well, so what? If she can have one or more orgasms *before* he does (and she can), and one or more *after* he does, why should it be important that she have one special orgasm at the precise moment he climaxes? But a problem does arise if either partner views the man's orgasm as the conclusion of everything. If the guy quits, withdraws, and rolls over, leaving her three steps from the top of the mountain, then that timing can be all important. She will have either to bring herself to orgasm or try to go to sleep with what could become an ache deep down within her. No gentleman would intentionally leave a lady in that condition, anymore than a lady would leave him in a similar state. And he doesn't have to.

Every woman knows, or should know, that most men would find it most uncomfortable to try going on with coitus after reaching orgasm, at least right away. And no gal with sense and consideration would imply that she expects him to. But that doesn't have to make it impossible for him to go on to satisfy her. At the moment the man reaches his climax, he reflexively penetrates her to the fullest. This is ordinarily deeply satisfying to both partners (and it is what makes withdrawal as a birth control method so frustrating and destructive). It is any continuing thrusting afterward which is uncomfortable, isn't it? It isn't irritating or uncomfortable to you just to stay all the way inside, not withdrawing until after she reaches orgasm (and not being in a hurry even then). What then you ask? Is just having you stay inside her enough to bring her to orgasm? Sometimes, if she was very close to it when you ejaculated, but probably not most of the time. She will need further stimulation. You might try stimulating her clitoris with your fingers if you are in position in which you can do so. You might also try another technique: If you stay fully penetrated and engage in a rocking movement, up and down with your shoulders rising over hers or in a side-to-side motion, you can give satisfying stimulation to her without experiencing discomfort. Even if for some reason (and I can't think of any offhand) you must withdraw before she reaches her climax, just remember there are several ways to bring a woman to the peak of sexual enjoyment. Some may be preferable to others, but she doesn't have to be left unfulfilled.

Impotence. This is a lousy word, as bad as the word "frigid." It's one of those words that spell failure and a lack of manhood. And really, what are we talking about when we toss that word around? We might be talking about a poor guy who can never attain or sustain an erection. But probably not. Usually, it just means that once in a while occurrence which happens to just about every guy who ever made love to a woman. Too bad it can't be left at that. And it could be if men could get their excessive hang-up on masculinity out of the way. Perhaps that's impossible. Men center so much of their self-image in their genital prowess. Unfortunately, it can set a man up for some real letdowns.

Stop and think about it. You don't have to have an

erection to make love to a woman and make her love you for the way you do so. You are more to her than that. If you think just of the time involved in love-making with a pair of accomplished lovers on one of those extra special big evenings, you have to conclude that that erection is really of big-deal importance only in the last few minutes. And even then it isn't crucial to her satisfaction. So let's say it is one of those nights when you have been beat down inside your shoe tops at the office and you couldn't get it up with an oyster dinner, a whirlpool bath, and a chorus of harem girls. Yet it is also one of those nights that your gal is not just willing and ready, she almost rips your suit off you when you walk through the door. Do you reach for the gin and do a collapse in front of the tube for the evening leaving her to her own resources? Not if you're a varsity letter man lover you don't. You don't cop out with a complaint of fatigue. You aren't all *that* tired. You can, after all, make love to her lying down. You have at least a half dozen ways in which to pleasure her. And aren't they all enjoyable to you?

If it happens frequently, however, you obviously are not going to be getting everything you want out of sex, so it is apparent you should do something about it if you can. And in most cases, you can. You might get some help from a psychologist or psychiatrist, but I don't think that's usually necessary. I'm sure it isn't, in most love affairs, some big psychological thing. It just needs to be seen through the colored glasses of common sense. Start by having a good loving talk with your gal. Unless both of you are able to look at it as simply something which can, and does, happen to nearly every couple—and to take all that "failure" nonsense out of it, you may build it into a major problem. Next, if it has happened rather frequently, try

one of two approaches. You might even try both. One
is described in a book by Dr. Joseph Wolpe.[1] The
other is a technique employed by Masters and Johnson at their sex clinic in St. Louis.[2] Both approaches
work, but better than that, they don't take months of
some sort of "treatment." Both call for cooperation
from the gal but no problem there; she gets pleasure in
the process. I'm not going even to try to describe the
techniques they suggest. In the first place, I'm not sure
I could do them justice, and furthermore, I don't want
to make this a chapter on "problems." I'm just tossing
in the suggestions in case they might be of some help.
But whatever you do, don't make it a major trauma. It
isn't the whole thing in love-making; it isn't even the
major thing as far as a woman is concerned. Keep
your ego out of it and you'll have more fun. And so
will she.

If She Is Unresponsive. What can I say about the
members of my sex who can't or won't turn on to sex
with their men? That I'm sorry? For them as well as
their men? Sure. Maybe some of them wouldn't have
the problem if they had been raised by mothers who
weren't all anti-sexual nuts. Most of the authorities
who have studied frigidity pin the blame on this kind
of mother. And from the gals I've talked with who
have a problem turning on, I'd have to agree with the
authorities. Frigid wives are not turned out by frigid
husbands as much as by frigid mothers. But that
doesn't mean that men have nothing to do with a gal's
lack of loving in a sexual sense. They do.

Becoming sexually responsive and reaching what

---

[1] Wolpe, J. *Psychotherapy by Reciprocal Inhibition.* Stanford: Stanford University Press, 1958.
[2] Masters, W. H. and Johnson, V. E. *Human Sexual Inadequacy.*
Boston: Little, Brown and Co., 1970.

can properly be called sexual fulfillment is a much tougher road for a gal than it is for a man. In fact, most of you men have it easy—at least when it comes to reaching an orgasm. For a gal to be able to make it at any time, she has to be able to accept herself and her own sexuality (in a mixed-up society which still sees sex as pretty much an all-male business). She also has to be able to let go of not only her inhibitions, but of her natural tendency to hold back and not "surrender" to a man. A marriage license is seldom, if ever, going to be enough to melt the thaw. You don't reverse years of conditioning with a piece of paper. In "letting go," she has to be able to rely on her man, to place all her trust in him. And that, lover, is a tall order. That gal of yours has to step off a cliff and rely on you to catch her. And she has to do it over and over again.

What if you don't catch her when she takes the leap? Ask most women you meet. They've been in such a spot. "I can't count on him; he's irresponsible." What an army of gals have chorused *that* complaint! Not all of it justified, I'm very sure. There are, I'll be the first to admit, a lot of very bitchy females wandering about. But let's agree that there are more than a few men who cop out on what their women have a right to expect from them. And does this result in unresponsive gals when they climb between the sheets? You better believe it.

In the next chapter I'm going to share one gal's insights into what we females hope to find when we climb out to the edge of that cliff. For now, however, I have a few suggestions for you in the event you find your gal isn't responding in the way you want—and certainly not in the way she wants—to your love-making:

1. I said this before, but it is important enough to repeat. Sex is important. Maybe not the most important thing in life, although I guess that might be argued. But it is important. No single sex experience, however, should ever be made the end of the world or the ultimate achievement in life. If she doesn't reach a climax when you make love, it's unfortunate, but she isn't going to fly into bits and pieces all over the bedroom unless she is already very unglued. So why should you?

2. Do not, by your words and actions, place your entire focus on that almighty orgasm. Don't treat her like a pushbutton robot—push the button and she has an orgasm. The gal's climax becomes, let's face it, a big ego trip for a lot of men, and they virtually demand that "it" happen (as if she doesn't have any interest in it herself) and if she doesn't have "it" happen to her, she has let her man down. There should be a lot of loving in love-making. An orgasm is only a part of it and if it doesn't happen, well, that doesn't wipe out all the fun of the love-making. Don't put her on the spot by asking her that test question designed to massage the male vanity, "Did it happen for you?"

3. Examine your love-making efforts. Are you communicating a desire for *her* or only a desire for sex? A woman wants her man to make love to her, not just go after "it." If you don't give your attention to the tenderness and romance which tell her *she* is important to you, that you love her and want her and want to please her, you are almost sure to strike out. Taking her for granted is the kiss of death. Too many men treat the love-making which I call "twoplay" as a sort of annoying necessity, a means to an end, and they go at it in a way which doesn't hide the fact. Then they wonder why their gals are less than passionate play-

mates. Well, I can tell them. A woman hungers for love, and it is her hunger for love which makes her hunger for sex. Being loved turns her on to sex. And feeling unloved turns her off. It's probably why there are few females interested in being served by even the most adept male prostitute. Without a feeling of genuine love, most gals would say, "Forget it." If you expect her to respond, love can't be something you turn on when you want sex and keep turned off at all other times. If we must be honest about it, most men, especially the married variety, are lousy lovers. And if you ask their women what makes them such losers you'll hear a string of complaints that adds up to a bundle of frustration with unloving men, guys who show affection only when they feel horny—and then not much. You may have loving feelings toward her, but she can't read your mind. If you don't express it with words and actions, she won't know it or feel it. If you are interested in having a responsive gal share your bed (and I assume you are or why else are you reading this book?), your love-making when you are *not* aiming toward sex is probably more important than your technique in bed.

After you evaluate your out-of-bed loving, pay some attention to what you're doing when you try to please her sexually. Remember, there are many ways to pleasure a woman's body. There are a number of places you can excite with your fingers and lips. In fact, if you use your hands and mouth with sensitivity, I can't think of any spot on a female's body that can't be pleasured to the edge of orgasm. Take enough time, do enough things to enough places on her body with enough attention to what she likes, and you will score high as a lover. Orgasm or no orgasm.

4. Break up those sexual habit patterns. If just

about every time you make love, you do it in the same place, at the same time, and probably in the same way, you may have one of those negative-response habit patterns built up. Believe me, it can happen. And it does happen in a surprising number of marriages. That house she keeps in running order can become a drag. She may have decorated it just the way she always wanted. It may give her a whole lot of satisfaction in many ways. But those four walls can still become a big bore. It may even have some negative associations. The kitchen with the garbage disposal that never works. The hard-to-clean carpet in the living room. The noise and nagging problems of children coming and going. The worries over the monthly bills. They all may have associations with that house. Not that she dislikes the house or the children or even the living room carpet, but they are at best only distantly associated with romance in the way a hotel room with you for the weekend is. Which is one reason why some gals who are off again on again responsive at home in the bedroom are passionate tigresses when away with their men. They may say it's because they are away from the responsibility of the children, and that may have something to do with it, especially for those "good mother" types who can't seem to resolve motherhood with sex, but there may also be a large component of boredom and negative associations tied up with the same old homey bedroom. Think back to the last few times you spent the evening with her in a hotel room or shacked up for the afternoon in a motel or made love in the back seat of the car. Was she more responsive those times than usual? If so, you may have an important clue to work with when it comes to injecting some essence of pure passion into your love affair. Try breaking up the bedroom-at-night routine and see if it doesn't make a difference.

5. Let her know you expect her to behave as a smart and skilled mistress should and would. She does have a choice, you know. The gal who says, "I know I just lay there like a statue; I just can't respond; I didn't feel anything," is telling herself lies. Of course she doesn't have to act like a chunk of granite. "But what if I don't feel anything?" is an evasive question. Neither sex can honestly use that excuse. Of course she feels something. Dig your fingernails into her fanny. You'll find out she is capable of feeling. But that's pain, she'll say. And what she means is that she doesn't feel anything sensual and erotic. Maybe not, but I still say she is perfectly capable of feeling good sensual feelings if—and it's a big *if*—she is willing to permit herself to. I'm not saying a gal can just *decide* to have an orgasm and *voilà!* But as I've said a few times or more, an orgasm isn't the ultimate goal in one's life—let's hope. And I am not talking of whether she reaches an orgasm each and every time. I am saying she does *feel*. And she is capable of moving and responding and doing all sorts of sensibly sexual activities. In a previous book, *How to Be a Happily Married Mistress,* a work obviously written for gals, I had a few things to say about women who choose to, at most, submit to sex but don't throw themselves into love-making with enthusiasm and gusto. And did I get the mail from outraged females (I'm a traitor to my sex, you see, if I try to suggest how blondes, brunettes, and redheads can have more fun). They said I was actually suggesting that if a gal didn't experience orgasm or even a high pitch of sexiness in love-making, she might be wise to fake it! Horrors! Maybe that is what

I said. I'm not going to spend time looking through the book to find out. But what is so horrible about that? They said I was suggesting they be dishonest or hypocritical. Nonsense! I was actually only suggesting that a gal should give to her man what she wants him to give her: *enthusiastic love*. If you discover she is in the mood for loving on an evening when sleep seems more appealing to you but you go ahead anyway, she isn't likely to be thrilled by the experience if you act bored and listless and slightly turned off while you are performing your "husbandly duty." And if you do ever act that way, you deserve the reaction you will probably get from her. I am not talking, in this case, of how either one of you may or may not *feel* at any particular time. I'm talking of how you *act* toward each other. How you *feel* is something only you can know. And only she can know what she may be feeling. But your feelings don't have to determine *your* actions. Or hers. So let her know what you want from her in sex. I don't mean tell her what you expect her to *feel*. You can't demand or control the feelings of your mistress. Tell her the *actions* you want. After all, if you paid a prostitute for a night in a hotel you would expect her to follow your lead and jump, squirm, and moan in just the right ways, wouldn't you? Well that gal of yours should have more motivation to do the same. She's getting more from you than a few bucks! What I'm suggesting here is in no way a put-down of my sex. It is actually as much for her benefit as it is for your pleasure. As a gal learns to act in a sexually responsive way, she begins to *feel* sexually responsive. And isn't that what she wants? If she waits for the feelings before the actions, the feelings may never come around. So you see, I really am on the side of my sex.

6. If she has had a long-standing problem of sexual unresponsiveness and she is willing to try to do something about it, there are a couple of things you might do to help. First, don't be critical or demanding. She didn't ask to be frigid and she doesn't like it anymore than you do. If you treat her like she's a freak or only half a woman, or if you act toward her as if she has chosen this way to punish or reject you, you are being grossly unfair. Furthermore, you will only make matters worse. She needs acceptance and love, not a little boy who acts like mother took away his ice cream cone. An orgasm is not something you can achieve by an act of will (anymore than an erection is). The more she "tries for it," in fact, the more illusive it is likely to become. She should be encouraged to put that almighty orgasm as far out of her mind as she can and simply join you in enjoying love-making. Too many people take sex far too seriously. It should be fun. And both partners should accept and enjoy the pleasures of what they are doing to and for each other each moment, without concentrating everything on whether that final orgasm is going to "happen."

You might also pick up the following books: *The Sensuous Woman* by "J" (Lyle Stuart, Inc., New York: 1969) and my book, *How to Be a Happily Married Mistress* (Doubleday & Co., Inc., Garden City, New York: 1970). Read them yourself before you give them to her. Perhaps they will give you a bit more understanding of what a gal is up against in this business of sexual responsiveness. Then tread lightly in giving her the books. If you've lived with her for a while, you should know her reactions pretty well, what she can accept and what she can't. The books are not written for prudes, male or female. And they don't have the answer for a gal who is living with an insensi-

tive, selfish slob who thinks only of his own ego grati-
fication when it comes to her response. But if you have
a good love affair going with your gal and you know
she is genuinely eager to do something about the situation and open-minded enough to take some necessary
steps (such as learning how to develop her sensuality
through masturbation, something she was taught is a
terrible no-no), the books can be given and received
in the right spirit: your attempt to help her bring more
joy into her life. Whatever you do, don't get on her
back about the whole thing and act as if you are the
self-appointed teacher who is going to shape up that
mixed-up female of yours. Don't even check on
whether she reads the books or ask her views on them.
If she wants to talk about them, that's up to her. Masters and Johnson describe some "exercises" they suggest at their sex clinic which can help a lot with some
gals. They call for some loving cooperation from the
male partner. If she wants to try them, fine. What
good lover would refuse? But let her initiate the "program," don't push her. The biggest job in overcoming
a lack of response is mental. Until she can straighten
out her own thinking about sex, about being female in
a male world, about the nature of surrendering not so
much to a man as to her own feminine sexuality, no
exercises will turn on her switches. Your biggest role
then is to love her well enough in every way that she
can learn that all those feminists, the women who have
raised her to resent men and to fight the tired old domestic battle of the sexes, were a bunch of harpies,
that it isn't at all the way they said—at least not in *her*
life.

In case she decides she cannot handle the problem
on her own even with the help of the books and her
lover, don't hesitate to suggest that the two of you seek

some professional help. And yes, I did say the two of you. Chances are you will be asked to come in by anyone she might go to for help. You are, after all, a big part of her life, and any probelm she has is your problem too; at least it should be.

Above all, give her lots of loving. Frigidity is almost another name for insecurity. The unresponsive gal is really a scared (or in some cases, hostile) little gal. She needs to be loved and feel loved if she is to develop the confidence and security to overcome these feelings. And don't forget: Loving means something more to a gal than just what goes on on a mattress. She wants to feel you want her because you love her, not just love her because you want her.

CHAPTER NINE

You Tarzan;
Me Jane

Some muscle-headed wag once said that a woman was like a Persian rug: She needs an occasional beating to keep her in good condition. Any nitwit who believes *that* belongs in a cage and needs a keeper. He sure shouldn't be wished on any woman. Except I must admit there are some women (not many) who seem to pant after guys who get their kicks from physically or verbally punching them around. What I'm going to say isn't for those kinds of males or their pathetic females. They belong with the leather and whips crowd. No thanks!

I make the point, however, because I can anticipate the reactions from the bra-burning babes who would resist giving a man—any man—their used dental floss and are forever dashing around with stringy hair trying to prove their independence, their "liberation" from the chains of a love affair with a man (some chains!). They will say I'm a masochist and/or accuse me of selling my sisters into bondage, a dreadful subservience to the chauvinistic males. Well, I'm not turned on by punishment and I don't subscribe to slavery. But I don't feel, either, that my sex is in any danger of being sentenced to any marital tiger pits. I happen to be firmly convinced that I have every bit as much opportunity to achieve anything I am capable and desirous of achieving as any man. So maybe I can't become a sergeant in the tank corps. And you can't get a job as a topless waitress. I'm sure not losing any sleep over it. Are you?

No, what I'm going to say won't apply to those hostile hussies. I'm talking (all the way through these pages) about normal turned-on-by-men gals, the kind you are hopefully sharing bed and board with. And those gals will have no argument with what I have to say. So here goes:

Women are *not* by nature (whatever that means) submissive, but when it comes to the man they love, they want to be able to submit. Maybe "submit" isn't the right word. It does, I suppose, seem a bit like running up a white flag, which sounds like there has been a war between the sexes. So instead, let's just say women want to be able to follow their men, not lead them. A few chapters ago I said a few things about this. Now I want to expand it and double the emphasis. It's something I hear all the time from women who are newly wed, girls who are dating high school boys, and middle-aged grandmothers. They all say the same thing: "I wish he would take over; not always expect me to make the decisions." And the other complaint: "He lets me push him around; I sometimes wish he would tell me to 'shut up.'"

I'm sorry to have to say it, but a whale of a lot of

men these days are really gutless. They were probably raised by mothers who performed psychological surgery on their fathers which had them singing soprano, mothers who kept the whole family in line with their manipulations and emotional mayhem. They grew up (if "grew up" is an appropriate description of their "development") with a pants-wetting fear of women. Then they married. Mistake number one. They knuckled under to a new "mother" who dominated them "just like the girl who married dear old dad" had done so well. But the gals they marry don't want the role of drill sergeant. No honest-to-God woman would. They get it by default, and they don't know how to get rid of it. And maybe they can't unless their men take the initiative and assume the masculine role which every normal gal looks for in a man.

Just what does a gal look for? It isn't easy to get an honest, straightforward answer to that question. For one thing, unless the gal has gotten the leadership from her man that she has yearned for (sometimes without being aware of her yearnings), she simply cannot come right out and admit that she wants him to lead the parade and set the tempo. To say it openly would be tantamount to saying, "Here, I'll let you take the reins," which of course would amount to telling him she was in charge but was willing to let him at least pretend he was leading. No, she doesn't want to push the leadership on him; she wants him to *take it.*

You know, I sometimes think every man should be given instructions in dog training. It might help him establish a "working" relationship with a woman. No, I'm not saying she's a dog or that you should treat her like a dog. But there are a few applications which might be useful. For one thing, a dog needs to know who is master. A woman needs the same thing. Your dog will never accept you as master if you show only an off-again-on-again concern and involvement or if you appear indecisive. Neither will your gal. And regardless of the "messages" she may have sent you in the past, she does want you to be the "master." She wants you to keep a firm hand on the tiller, or, in dog-training parlance, a firm hand on the choke chain. Oh, not that she is looking for a petty autocrat. She sure isn't. Nor does she need someone to tell her when to blow her nose and change her panty hose. So what does she want? She wants limits. And authority. And responsibility. And leadership. All from her man.

I don't know when we started getting so mixed up in our approach to how men and women should relate to one another when they set out to build what they hope will be a beautiful thing. But I'm sure it wasn't always like this. Somewhere along the line somebody, undoubtedly a female, got the idea that men and women could make it better if they "related to each other as equals." A good liberal cause, what? Except for one thing: the concept of *equality* took an awful beating. The gals ended up on top; the men ended up three feet tall; and both sexes ended up living a life of fatalistic frustration.

I'll make the point again: Sure I believe in equality of the sexes, but I don't want to be a man. And I sure like the idea of having the sexes *separate* but equal, *different* but equal. I say keep the roles distinct with men as men and women as women. And I'll lay odds most gals will agree.

About the only place you run into the title "head of the household" any more is on the income tax report. And what will you bet the women's libbers will get that scrapped unless it applies only to females. But show me a *happy, satisfied* gal who doesn't enjoy having her man take the lead.

You hear it all the time. Ask a couple, "Who makes the major decisions?" They'll tell you they "talk things out together." Now I ask you, could anyone come up with a less efficient way to run a circus? Why in the world do you need two people to make all those decisions? If they have only half a brain apiece, maybe they can only make it if they pair up. But if you each have something other than dried snails between your ears, do you need a vote on all these rinky-dink matters?

Of course that doesn't mean that the command scepter of leadership *must* be carried by the male of the species. It's just that we gals like it that way—at least in the matters which we see as masculine (sex, for example). That doesn't mean we want our men to tell us when to clip our toenails and how to balance a checkbook. And it doesn't mean we can't make the decisions without help if we have to. But do we have to? Not if we have men with balls.

Any intelligent member of my sex is rationally lazy. Why should she poke her fingers into somebody else's pie if all she will come out with is sticky fingers? Why should I have to handle the finances if he will? And if I simply keep hands off the money matters, he'll have to take over. And I'd much rather not dash around consulting with travel agents and such if my man is willing to plan the vacations.

I have no interest in checking out which new car on the market gives the best mileage or which savings and loan pays top interest rates. My natural laziness keeps me from phoning for dinner reservations, pushing my man up the ladder of success, or sitting in on meetings with the agent who sells him insurance. These things are all pieces of the jigsaw puzzle of his world. I leave it to him to fit them together and keep them from falling apart. He's a man, all man. He doesn't need my help to do his thing.

He wants me to be his woman. And I like it that way. I guess you could call me a "kept woman." And the accusation doesn't bother me a bit. I recently read an article by that commandant of the army of frigid feminists Betty Friedan, in which she made some confused point about how hard some of her "sisters" were working at liberating themselves, taking jobs or returning to college, from the slavery of morning appointments at the beauty salon and afternoons of pampering themselves while they await their men. Go to it, Betty baby, but count me out. I enjoy a beautiful freedom from guilt feelings in this area. I don't feel I have to get out and peddle cosmetics door-to-door to "do my part" if my man is happy having me as his "kept woman." And I don't hold any doubts which compel me to march off to take a Ph.D. in order to prove something called my potential to myself (or anyone else). You're damn right he's the center of my life. (Friedan would call that "the problem that has no name." Too bad poor Betty doesn't enjoy such a "problem.") He likes supporting me; he isn't resentful that I may spend an afternoon doing things with bath oils and perfumes. It's for him, and I make sure he knows it. Is he a male chauvinist? You'd better believe it. Show me a man who isn't, and I'll show you a loser in the chase for a turned-on woman.

Don't think this means I have nothing to do all day but lie around on my satin sheets or chase around gulping coffee with the pin-curl set. If we are going to do our thing together, I have to make sure I do my own thing with all the efficiency and feminine vigor I can muster. I don't need his direction in keeping up my corners of the castle. I don't tell him how to handle his responsibilities; he doesn't tell me how to handle mine. I take it for granted he will keep up his end, and if I want to keep my man, and keep him happy, I better keep up mine.

How does it work? Just great! For me and for every other gal I've talked with lucky enough to be living the life. And I have heard no complaints from their men—and they *are* men. But one thing is certain: It doesn't come about without a great and glorious hassle!

There is one thing about women you don't have to be told: We can be contrary, stubborn, and we don't often fight fair. You learned that an eon ago, probably from the first gal you dated (which proves something about the power of hormones since men still end up marrying women). There is another thing, however, which you may not know: A whole lot of that stubborn bitchiness is really the gal's attempt to test the limits. It works something like this: She meets a guy who turns her on. She falls for him—hard. And when she falls, it means that she wants to share his bunk and breakfast for all time all the time. And at that point, to repeat what I said a few pages back, she has to face a decision about jumping off a high cliff with hopes her man will catch her. That, lover, doesn't come easy. Just ask any woman. Naturally, she wants to buy some insurance, to up the odds in her favor. So she feels her lover's muscles to make sure he has what it takes to keep her from splattering on the rocks and shoals. She checks to see that he has balls. And how does she do it? With that contrary bitchiness of hers. She pushes; she demands; she manipulates. She pulls every trick of temper, guile, and petulance she learned in the sorority of conniving females. She pushes, probes, and shoves into and on her man, hoping that her pushing can go just so far and no further, that at some point she will run smack up against a brick wall—a man she can't budge. Once she finds she can go just so far and no further, she can relax. He'll catch her. He will become the solid brick wall she can lean against.

That, lover, is where it's at. She wants to find that brick wall in *you*. And if she doesn't? If she finds she can lead you around by the ring through your nose? Then you can count on only two results. First, she isn't going to melt for you the way you want her to. She will stay tense and testy, and who needs that? Certainly not *you*. Second, she will keep up the testing. She'll demand. She'll bitch. She'll nag. Given the chance, she'll do a pretty effective job of castrating you in a dozen different ways. If you can't, or won't pull up on that choke chain, she'll run all over you.

How do you do it? Well, admitting that you may have some undoing to go through if you have let the whole thing get out of hand, you have to start with a hard, hard look at what you have been doing, or not doing. If you've been sucking your thumb where she is concerned, indulging your masculine desires without much regard for her, you're going to have to put your little boy gears in reverse. Face up! She wants to be *cherished*. If she is, she'll follow you through a mansion of mad mice. That means, and make no mistake about it, that she better be sure she comes number one on your list of priorities. It works both ways. You want her to place you ahead of everything and everybody else. And she wants to feel she holds a similar position with you. You want to take the lead, make the decisions? Then lead for her, make the decisions in

ways which express your love. If you plan the dates,
but each time your only question is, "Where do I want
to go?" don't expect to exercise that male prerogative
for long. A *man* handles the finances in his family. He
doesn't pass the buck to his spouse. But he uses the
money and assumes the responsibility for her and his
family, not his own indulgence. If there is one guy
who will turn off a gal and keep her turned off, it's
the clown who figures that because his name is on the
pay check the money is his to spend as he pleases,
strictly for himself. If his gal is to have anything for
herself, she will have to go out and get a job, and even
then, he will probably demand she turn the money
over to him. Every true leader serves those who follow
him. If you serve her needs and desires and place
them above your own, she will be happy to turn over
the finances to you. And hopefully, you will be man
enough to handle them. And that goes for leadership
in the other important areas of your life together.
Don't forget, however, that she has responsibilities
also. If you treat her like a little kid and instruct her
and supervise her in everything she is expected to do,
or do it all for her, you won't be very satisfied and neither will she.

As for that choke chain, let me try to spell out what
I mean by it and how it works. A firm tug on the
choke chain catches the dog up short and says, "That's
as far as you go, now shape up." If used effectively,
the dog learns quickly that staying quietly in line is not
only the smartest but the most satisfying. Is the choke
chain a form of punishment? Yes and no. If the limitations of the choke chain have been learned, it obviously won't be punishing since it won't be yanked. But if
the dog has been in the habit of lunging and following
his own lead, then that sharp tug may be a bit uncom-

fortable until the lesson is learned. And gals are no different. A gal may choke once or twice when you start snapping her into line behind your lead, but if you go about it right, she will soon learn to relax and enjoy it. It's really what she wants, regardless of how much of a struggle she may put up at the start. Once you have her broken to a choke chain, you don't have to keep struggling. You can also relax.

(Now I can sit back and wait for the feminists to ride in on their brooms to burn one of those female sex symbols on my front lawn.)

The first step comes in knowing why and when you want to pull up on a choke chain. In other words, you better know what you believe in, what you stand for, what you are willing to accept and not accept, and what terms you are willing to establish for the "contract" of the relationship with that gal of yours. If a man doesn't know where he stands, and what he will stand for, he can't expect his woman to know. No way! You know what you want from her. At least you should know. But does she? Or perhaps more important, does she know where you draw the line, the point where you say, "This is all I'll tolerate; step over the line, and it's over between us." That's what I mean by the terms of the contract. A relationship which has no conditions, where they each accept one another regardless of how much flap they may give each other, is pathetic. Some nut came along years ago with the notion that we should accept others as they are. It sounds so nice and tolerant, doesn't it? And we are supposed to be tolerant. It's so charitable and cultured. And if we are talking about a man and woman making a life together, it's so *dumb!* It means if I find myself with a guy who stays tied to his mother, or can't hold a job, gets his kicks rapping me in the mouth, or spends his time hanging out in gay bars, I'm supposed to live with it and like it—or at least put up with it. Not I, lover. There are many things I enjoy having a man do to me. Torture isn't included. I'll set my limits and conditions and I expect him to do likewise. If he can tell me, "Look, I want to live with you, but only under the following conditions," then I can know where I stand and make my choice—either-or.

So let her know just where you set the limits. And don't act as wishy-washy as the majority of males. Nagging, bickering, shouting, or coaxing are fruitless attempts to establish a man-woman oneness. And if she doesn't go along with the limits? Well, that depends on how important it is. It seems to me there are some things a man cannot ignore or tolerate and still stay a man either to himself or his woman. Being second tops the list, and it doesn't make much difference what or who he may be second to. My man wants to be first in my life above any job, hobby, kids, friends and relatives, and other men. It doesn't make much difference to him (or to me, for that matter) whether somebody might say it's fair or unfair, fifty-fifty or ninety-ten, black or white. All I have to decide is whether I want him enough to pay the price—whatever the price may be. No arguments. No compromises. (By the same token, I also have a price in terms of conditions. He has to decide whether to meet it.)

And what if she won't go along? I know one guy who is very much a man. He laid it firmly on the line for his woman. "I want to fly," he told her, "and I want to fly high with you beside me; just don't crap on my tail feathers." If she ever drags her heels in following him, she'll find herself in a solo bed and she knows it. It's the ultimate choke chain, and the most rational one. If she wants you around the hearth and boudoir but figures you will be until death do one of you part regardless of how much she walks on your plans, dreams. and virility, what's going to get her off her femine smugness? The answer is Nothing. One poor sad dope told me he "hoped" his chilly-bitchy frau would change "someday" but that if she didn't, he would still never consider packing up and taking off. "I did marry her for better or for worse and if it all turns out to be for worse, well I guess I just live with it." Maybe that makes sense to him, but not me. If a tree falls on me and I end up in a wheel chair for life, I'm sure my man will be by my side, just as I would stick by him and love him if the positions were reversed. But I'm not living with a fool. Why should he hang on and put up with a woman who refuses to give him what will satisfy him? If he were that stupid, I'm not sure I'd find many kicks in living with him. So long as I continue to be the woman he wants and the gal who can pleasure him in all the ways he looks for, I don't fear any competition or the door closing behind him. If that's the choke chain he holds, it's a pretty effective one. I know; I hold one too.

When I called that the ultimate choke chain, I meant it. And that means no games, no bluffs. There are not many games much sicker than the "maybe we ought to separate" game. You know the parrying, don't you? Some couples play it out every week or so. They hassle each other over whatever they can find to mold into a bloodletting session. Then, right on cue, one of them comes out with that let's split up line. It brings down the curtain on the second act and opens act three. They play word games around the theme of how they divide the color slides of the Grand Canyon and who gets custody of the tropical fish. When they tire of the game, it's time for one of them and then the other to call a halt with, "I don't want to leave you, etc., etc., ad nauseum." It's a game designed for a playpen. If two adults are going to part company, they should do so as adults, which means go ahead and do so. Threats, and games disguised as threats, get nobody anywhere. If anything, they just serve to convince both partners that the mutual misery, like the music, will go 'round and 'round—forever.

I better jump in here, I guess, and make a clarifying point before you get the idea I'm promoting a mass exodus from my sex by your sex every time my sex slips off the narrow line of loving behavior. If you walk out every time she ends up on the other side of a viewpoint, you had better get an apartment with a revolving door and an endless supply of gullible gals. That final solution isn't any answer to the everyday question of how do you get her to follow your lead. Who would you have to lead after you've left?

You do have other choke chains to bring her into line. Sex is one most men would never think of. And let me say right now I think it's really a vicious weapon. Sex should be for making love, not war. But there are times when drastic situations call for drastic measures. Women have been taught to use sex as a choke chain for all past generations, so maybe some poetic justice is deserved. Remember Lysistrata talking her fellow women into withholding their sexual "favors" until their men agreed to quit warring? What she started! Women have been using what they seem to think is gold-plated to get what they want ever since. They dangle sex like a carrot before the jackass, and let the jackass fail to cater to their momentary whim and just that quick the carrot disappears. O.K., if she has pulled that "not tonight" jazz more than a few frustrating times for no good reason (and what's a good reason other than an illness that really wipes you out), maybe it's time to play the same choke chain game. Withdraw *your* sexual favors. Sure. I'm serious. Every gal has been raised to expect the game to be played only one way. A man, she was taught, is always after her tempting body, regardless of how she acts in bed or out of bed. If he forgets to shave before retiring, or doesn't buy her the new washing machine, or if she suffers a headache or a case of athlete's foot, it's no-no tonight. How often does a man play turn about? You're right. Probably never. Probably sixty per cent of the men living with women are sure their women would never miss it and would be just as happy being left alone. I'm sure some of them are not mistaken (I've met their women—brrr!), but the great big majority of gals have bodies and warm blood and hot desires. And they dig loving. If their men cut it off, they would suffer. Men don't believe it because they never test to find out.

If you decide to withhold the sexual advances, do so with a plan. If you take an "I'll be damned if I give her any loving tonight" approach, you are simply indulging in a tit-for-tat, and she can easily see it for what it is. She can also hold out, remember. And if you sleep on the couch in a fit of annoyance, she can live with it. But what if you don't respond with a fit of pique? What if, in fact, you don't make an issue of cutting off the sexual favors, don't even mention what you plan to do? The results may surprise you. You may discover that a gal who acted all along like she could take it or leave it, can't really remain so cool and detached when her goodies are cut off. But don't do it with hostility. Remember those gag signs that say, "Love your enemies; it will drive them crazy." Well, the idea is something like that. Not that she is

your enemy, but the point to keep in mind is that you
are not going into a period of angry celibacy. You stay
pleasant, attentive, friendly, and even affectionate in a
non-sexy way. You just don't follow through. What do
you suppose her reaction will be when you climb into
bed *sans* pajamas (is there any way to sleep except in
the altogether?) very much erect and ready for the
third night in a row and tenderly kiss her good night,
roll over and go to sleep? One guy who carried out the
plan told me what happened. For a long time, his gal
had been pulling that "I'm tired; must we do it again
tonight?" routine. At the same time he quit making a
nightly pitch, he became even more the attentive lover; pleasant, interested, helpful, and all the rest. He
didn't tell her he had sworn off; he just didn't show
any interest in amorous pursuits. After three or four
days of this, she began making a few overtures of her
own, coming up and nibbling on his ear while he
watched TV, running her fingers through his hair
while he drank his afterdinner coffee, brushing her
hair in the nude before climbing into bed. A couple of
days of this with no results and she was ready for a
more aggressive approach. The kids were in bed. He
was ensconced in his reclining chair before the television set. She had been off in the bedroom for almost
an hour. When she walked in the room, she was wearing a soft pink negligee he had given her a year or so
before. Every freckle and curly hair on her body was
as visible as near-transparency could make it. Whatever she hoped for, it wasn't his response. He invited her
to sit down and watch the Late Show with him. The
following day was Saturday. She sent the kids off to a
movie. He was busy trying to set a new washer in the
leaky kitchen fauct she had complained about (for
over a month). This time, she called him to come into

the bedroom. He found her lying on the bed wearing nothing but a few strategically placed drops of perfume. Her greeting was decidedly that of a new woman: "Damnit! Get your clothes off. I want it bad!"

He saved the talking for later. But while they were enjoying a long Saturday afternoon aftermath lying side by side he let her know her game of holding back was over. From now on, there was going to be an era of equality and that she would be expected to get with it and start acting like a woman, not a prudish virgin. She got the message. And who can say who benefited most from the choke chain from then on?

The whole principle of the choke chain when it comes to getting a gal to follow her man and giving him the loving he wants is this: She has to want what he alone can give her, and she has to fear losing it. If she doesn't fear losing whatever he's got, he has no choke chain. And at that point, it's all over but the property settlement. Do I fear that man of mine? No, not really. I have never had reason to fear *him*. But I do fear making him unhappy with me. When that happens, I know he will be angry, and when he's angry, I know it. He doesn't holler or raise hell or stomp out or clobber me. But I know it. His face goes cold, and his silence communicates very well. But I don't even fear his facial expression. It is the loss of closeness. He gives me a warmth, affection, and the feeling of being a sensuous woman. If he cuts that off, my world goes dead. And *that* is what I fear. Even five or ten minutes of that sort of deadness is a horrible eternity. It gives him a very strong choke chain. Make your woman fall in love with you, keep her that way, and build it up continually, and you have the choke chain that's unbreakable.

When all is said and done, however, I would have

to place heavy weight on decisiveness and aggressiveness when it comes to getting a woman in love to follow her man. If she is turned on to him, then he can keep her his willing and responsive woman, ready to provide him more pleasures than a harem of creative nymphs, if he is willing to let her know what he expects of her and gutsy enough to persevere in going after it. Whoever said "Faint heart n'er scored with a real gal" or something like that knew what he or she was talking about. If you give up just because she "doesn't want to talk about it anymore," you are going to lose that leadership. If you let her run everything because "she does a better job of it," forget the hopes of having her your *woman;* she'll become your mother.

Jane may have known more about everything from literature to nuclear physics to Emily Post, but Tarzan called the shots. He knew what he wanted and let her know it. She knew what she wanted: Tarzan. Once that was cleared up, they had a swinging old time together. Jane had to break with the girls in the bridge club in doing so, and if your gal decides to follow her man, she too will find herself drummed out of the corps of suburban house fraus with their velour bathrobes and chastity belt mentalities. She will follow a different drummer. And you'll own the drum.

CHAPTER TEN

Who Are
All Those People
in My Bedroom?

Some years back, the advertising industry discovered something called "togetherness." They found they could use it to sell back yard barbecues, private campgrounds, and block party fireworks supplies. About the same time, the promoters of every cause this side of the League to Eliminate Dandruff began playing on guilt feelings we might never have had without the mass media pushing the virtue of community involvement. Other Madison Avenue types sold easy-to-operate cameras for the holidays with full-page spreads of Grandpa, Grandma, children, Mom, Dad, and Uncle Charlie gathered in boundless joy 'round the Christmas tree. And finally, along came the sensitivity session freaks. They borrowed heavily from the Haight-Ashbury flower children (circa 1966) in a "let's all join hands and dance around the Maypole" groupiness. They found almost overnight success in attracting adult men and women to scout camp wooded environments where they could all practice "awareness" on a mass and massed scale, jumping, squeezing, touching, leaping, singing, swearing, embracing, revealing, and, above all, RELATING. Middle-aged businessmen, mothers of three, goal-less college students, and avant-garde clergy stripped to the buff and rolled around on the floor in a sexless excess of communal rapport. The churches, the schools, and the commuters on the 5:17 found a new outlet for their primitive urges to gather the tribe around the warm fire of mutual support: Every gathering became a "community." Whee!

I recently glanced through one of those magazines for brides. The back pages of this journal for maidens anticipating marriage were filled with ads for honeymoon resorts (on the assumption, of course, that today the bride picks the honeymoon spot). If you have the idea that a honeymoon locale should be a place where two can split from the maddening throng and discover something beautiful in a timeless, romantic week or two, forget it. Honeymoons, from what the ads say, are designed for glorious groupiness. These castles in the Catskills come with oh-so-active social directors who make sure you don't feel out of it: bridge tournaments, hikes, folk dancing classes (I kid you not!), and even separate planned activities for the boys who miss getting together with just the boys. The only thing I can't figure is why they split the couples up into double rooms. Why not have them all sleep in a dorm?

If there is one thing a love affair doesn't need it's other people hanging around. Whatever group sex is besides a meeting of bored freaks, it isn't a love affair. And the last time I saw anything resembling a love affair going on at a cocktail party was in one of those eyes-meeting-across-a-crowded-room scenes in a 1930s film. It doesn't happen on a double date, or a vacation with friends, or a weekend with relatives, or a neighborhood barbecue, or a bridge party, or a dinner party for the boss, or a PTA meeting, or any other gathering in which you wind up with some friends or enemies (and in this context they are just about the same) between you and that gal of yours. Love affairs are for *two*. Add a third and you can have a triangle. With a fourth, you can play tennis doubles. But that one-to-one love affair goes on the shelf. And that's not for *this* gal. I hope it isn't for you.

Somebody, I'm sure, is going to write to me to tell me I'm advocating life in an ivory tower. And I'm not going to cop out. Show me the ivory tower with reasonable rent and a long-term lease, a six-foot square sunken tub, mirrored bedroom, and a moat around the property and I'll sign on the line. I'll never understand the perpetually involved do-gooders who are forever telling me, "You can't live in an ivory tower," as if life on a desert isle or in an ivory tower is immoral strictly because it is appealing. What rot! If that ivory tower of my dreams isn't falling on someone or polluting the atmosphere or some such, why can't I live in it? Alas, without the millions of a J. Paul Getty, ivory towers are pretty much out of the question. The beachcomber-on-a-desert-isle role has some appeal, but I'm sort of hooked on indoor plumbing and martinis over the rocks so that's out. No ivory tower. No desert isle.

But I can at least take the next best approach: I can keep most of those people out of my love affair and out of my bedroom most of the time. I know one thing: I can't love that man of mine the way he likes to be loved if I'm sharing my attentions with others. And I don't care who the others may be. It just can't be done. By me. By you. Or by that gal of yours.

I don't want to single out any particular somebodies who may be invading your loving pad, but I think some common invaders deserve special consideration, if for no other reason than the fact that they may be so difficult to fight off.

Relatives, yours or hers, should rank near the top of the list. You want to have the romance go flatter than yesterday's beer? Have Mother, yours or hers, parked in the adjoining bedroom. You may be uninhibited enough to give the bedsprings a good workout while mother is toying with her insomnia next door, but your bed partner may not be quite that free. Few gals are.

But the relatives don't have to live with you to dampen your romance. They can be in the bedroom psychologically as well as physically. The results are as disastrous one way as the other. Every gal with her head intact takes seriously those words about forsaking all others. She wants to know she is number one in the life of that man of hers. And that means ahead of his mother, father, sister, brother, Aunt Eloise, and assorted ex-girl friends. I know one young couple who learned this the hard way. They lived together for a couple of years while in college without "benefit" of marriage. During all that time, the parents of both avoided them as if they had a social disease, no visits, dinner invitations, or phone calls. Then they made it legal, and you can guess what happened. Right. The parents jumped into the in-law role with both feet. Holidays together. Sunday dinners. Motherly advice on everything from furnishing the apartment to family planning. A year after the nuptials, the kids were ready for the divorce court. Sure, they had done a few other dumb things to help bring on the breakup, such as becoming a very much "settled down" married couple with every dull thing that implies, but the eager fingers of the parents grubbing around in their relationship played a big, big part in it.

Everything I say about invading relatives goes double if the relative is female. We gals are green-eyed cats with sharp claws. The gal who isn't a viciously jealous feline when it comes to *her* man either isn't normal or doesn't care much about him. And it doesn't make it a different matter just because the "other woman" happens to be his mother, a daughter, or a ninety-year-old aunt who's a nun. Bring another female on the scene and you've just lit a cigar in a fireworks factory. No household has room for more than one female unless the other one is a daughter of the one who is number one—and knows it. And even then, watch out. If the other woman is the guy's mother, you can add fifty points to the problem. A gal wants—needs—to see her man as a man—all man, and her man. If she watches him behave like "Mother's little man" each time Mom is on the scene, she can forget the whole thing. She is going to see him shrink a foot or two and regress to age ten. He may not think he changes when his mother comes around, but maybe he should ask the gal he's living with. If she is honest, she will tell him. Better yet, don't ask. Just keep the relatives at a good arm's distance—a long, long arm.

This can be sticky, to say the least, if you have relatives living in the same town and/or you've established the practice of family get-togethers and that sort of thing. It may call for some gutsy decisions on your part, but then, isn't that what manhood's all about? If you don't want to make cutting off the relatives harder on yourself, there is one thing to watch out for: Don't get yourself in debt to them. If you use good old Mom for baby-sitting for three or four years, to then declare her *persona non grata* is a kick in the teeth. And that also goes for borrowing money from the folks, letting them help out with the down payment on the house, and similar subtle ways of going into hock to the blood-is-thicker-than-water establishment.

If they are her relatives who are crawling out of the woodwork, you have your troubles stacked just as high, but you may not be able to take as direct an approach. If you try changing the locks on the door or writing a "Don't call us; we'll call you" letter to your in-laws, you may discover just how chilly your gal can become—or how volatile. They are her parents. Leave the responsibility for cutting them off at the pass in her lap. And after the two of you have talked it out like a pair of grown-ups and she still won't cut the cord, what do you do then? Well I suppose you might throw in the towel and resign yourself to living it that way. You may end up with a perpetual little girl who will never give you the riches a real woman has to offer, but that's your choice. If that isn't good enough for you, then let me make a couple of suggestions. First, make sure you've broken away from your own parental traps. You can't expect to get far asking her to break away if you haven't. Then, be sure you are ready to give her whatever she was trying to get from clinging to her parents. Maybe it was security. Maybe companionship. Maybe love. And maybe they're all the same. But whatever she was after, a concerned lover can fill in any gaps that might result.

If she is tied to them with feelings of obligation ("I

owe my parents so much for everything they've done for me."), you may run into a higher stumbling block. Those feelings of indebtedness are hard to put down. Try having some rational conversations over the whole matter. And use patience. Don't expect her to become 100 per cent yours with the magic of a few words.

There are scores of other people who can play a hand in eroding away the great thing the two of you might have. In fact, just about anybody and everybody in the phone book can get past the front gate and between you and your woman if you let them—or don't fight them off. If you're an inmate in the corporation squirrel cage, those omnipresent business associates may be more than an annoyance to her; they may be as welcome as a migraine.

Back in the sweatshop days of the robber barons, the boss expected his two pounds of flesh and sixty hours of toil each week, but that was all. He didn't expect his white collar slaves to stop for a couple of drinks after work, join the office bowling league, or play golf with the prize account on that Saturday morning when plans had been made for a weekend away with the guy's long-suffering gal. You did your work and you got your pay. No fringe benefits and no fringe company socializing. Then the company brass read some sociology books and got hyped-up on the idea of turning the boys around the water cooler into one big happy "family" (when they weren't babbling about them being a "team"). This may have given the company what it hoped for ("Don't worry, J.B. won't accept that other job; he's captain of the bowling team."), but it surely has fouled up many a love affair. There are not too many gals who will happily share their man with a mistress. Some may be willing to put up with it for whatever they get from it by way of bed and board, but not this gal, and for her sake, I hope not your woman. And that job of yours can be every bit as much a mistress as another female. You may not look at it that way, but can you be sure she doesn't?

What about those chummy gatherings with the boys from the office when the wives are along? You know the sort. The drinks are poured and in less than five minutes the men are on one side talking shop and office politics. The women are on the other gabbing about kids, house, and other equally exciting matters. Now who, I ask you, but a group of cretins could get any jollys out of that? A cub pack of boys who don't dig girls, and a group of bored (maybe boring) girls they dragged along. I'm sure ordering a double order of pepperoni on their pizza is the most exciting thing some of those couples ever do. If they've got anything going for the two of them, or want anything, why are they there?

I've heard a lot of men say these booze and cold-cuts gatherings are essential to the job, or at least to "getting ahead." When I hear it, something inside says, "Nonsense." If a guy really has a lot of moxie and does his job better than anyone else, does he really have to play the social game in order to advance? Not unless he has a boss who is bound for bankruptcy. (If you do have that kind of boss, wouldn't it be wise to bail out before you go down with him?) The smart boss is going to go on ability, not party game skills. And as for that time dishonored custom of a drink with the boys before coming home, where can you find anything better for smashing a gal's dreams of a loving lover? Give this some thought: A woman who really loves a man wants to believe her man misses her when they are apart as much as she misses him. It's all a matter of priorities. If you stop with the boys, the boys are obviously more "appealing" than she is, at least for a time. Then how do you convince her she turns you on the most and that you are forever eager to be with her? The answer, of course, is that you can't. And where does that get you, lover? Nowhere. If you want her to greet you with wet lips and warm passions, show her you suffer from the same pangs of anticipation. And show it by being there, with your eager virility and concern for your gal, as soon as you have the chance. And whenever you have the chance.

You may have one of those jobs and one of those bosses which bring about a forced integration of business and social life. Some companies are convinced they can sell their product only if they oil the client with Scotch and dull his senses with rare steak. It really is part of the job. A sensible gal can understand that and accept it. But she isn't a fool. Don't try to con her into believing that playing liar's dice in a saloon with your buddies four nights out of five is part of the job. She'll know. I don't know how women can tell, but you better believe they can. If you have to be away from her, she can live with it and eagerly await your arrival, but she doesn't want leftovers.

Beyond those sticky "obligations" to relatives and employers, what about those involvements where you have a clear choice? Take, for a prime example, the "night out with the boys." This used to be promoted like vitamins and dental checkups. A man needs it, the marital sages said. And good wife-mothers went along with it. I think they felt it was necessary to a little boy's mental health or something. It took a while before a night out with the girls became popular with women and they started talking about the need for "girl talk." Just like junior high school days! I don't know about these types. As far as I'm concerned, I discovered the opposite sex long before the first high school dance and I found out how much fun they could be. Even more fun than girls. And I learned that all that business about guys and gals not talking the same language is so much bleep. And the idea that they don't share the same interests is so much of the same. If they can't find things to talk about and don't share interests, how did they get together in the first place? All those September jokes about football widows increases my adrenalin output. I can be as rabid a fan as my man and I can compare a scrambling quarterback with one who throws from the pocket with any group of guys. And at seven card stud, I'm ruthless. Sure I'm interested in women's fashions. I'm also interested in new styles for men. Since he has definite tastes in the clothes he likes to see me wear, my man is also interested in women's fashions. In conversation, activities, and you-name-it, I can give my man everything some other man can give him. And I have a few "extras" to offer.

The couples I have seen who play this never-the-twain-shall-meet separation game all seem to have one or another hang-up going against them: Either they stay so insulated from the world of their partner they have nothing to talk about and couldn't seemingly care less, or they have a neurotic thing about their "sexual identities." She won't take up fishing and football watching because "they're for men." He won't take her to a ballet because he doesn't want to look like a sissy. So he goes off with the boys, she goes with the girls, and the love affair goes down the drain.

I could say a few things to the gals who won't join their men. But I already have, and this book is for you men. When you play the *boys-will-be-boys-doing-*

their-masculine-thing game, you don't touch up your male image in her eyes. Not one bit. You lose points as a lover, and make no mistake: it will show up in her absence of amorous interest.

Everything I can say about double dating as a yeack non-romantic scene goes triple for a foursome (or more) vacation. I'd rather spend the time having my gall bladder removed. If you want to keep her interested in being alone with you in the bedroom, show her you want to be alone with her when you take her away —for a week or a weekend.

Now for the big question: If you have children, how do you keep them from crawling all over the two of you and breaking up those great moments together?

Take a consensus of parents and you'll find most of them are firmly convinced you can't do a thing about it; when kids come along, the honeymoon ends. You lose your privacy. You no longer have the time to spend together. And besides, parents don't act like lovers. Do they? Well, *do they?* Not if you observe most of the moms and dads on your block.

Well I'm a rebel. So is that man of mine. We don't buy the notion that kids have to mark the finish to our love affair. Keeping it active, however, does call for some adjustments. There are adjustments in time, place, need for privacy, etc. But first, it seems to me, there are some "adjustments" which need to be avoided. It has to do with image. When a family comes along, the guy and his gal start to see themselves in a different way. She is now a MOTHER. He is a FATHER. And these are more than just roles. They are images. *Mothers* don't wear bikini panties and join their lovers in a bubble bath. They don't go off on no-clothes-on weekends with their men or plan late night champagne dinners for two. *Fathers* play ball with their sons, but they don't make out in the back seat of a car with their son's mother. They don't sit on a beach with their gal and watch the sunset. Those activities are for lusty singles—or maybe for philandering spouses. But for good sensible parents? Not on your wedding pictures!

Well to hell with that image! If that's what parenthood demands, I'm all for population zero for every couple, starting with my own loving happening. But you can forget it. I know it doesn't have to take that route. You can have a whole houseful of children without it dampening the fires the two of you have blazing away one bit. In fact, keeping those flames high is one of the nicest things you can do for your kids as well as yourselves. They most certainly *don't* need parents who live in an emotional mausoleum.

Questions of time and place can be answered with a little thought and planning. And sometimes a firm stand and even firmer resolve. With little people wandering around the homestead, you can't very well dance in the altogether in the living room in the middle of the afternoon unless you're nudists. And you may have to wait until the offsprings are in bed before taking that shower for two. You no longer have that freedom to do swinging things together where and when the two of you have some new ideas and familiar urges. But let's face it. Who ever has anything approaching total freedom? Making love in the first-class lounge of a 747 sounds like the greatest way to spend an hour or two while you're up their circling in a holding pattern over Kennedy International, but I'm sure the FAA has some regulation about it even if it's only for seat belts (bureaucrats are as sexy as a deodorant ad). I have a great spread of lawn in the back yard and making beautiful things happen with the tingle of grass on your bare skin is a real sensual turn-on, but I have neighbors and a low fence, so what do I do? I keep the clothes *on* my back and the law *off*. Those limitations on my freedom weren't imposed by children, and I've learned to live with *them*. So I certainly can learn to live with those that come with kids. Children *do* go to bed and they can be outlasted, can't they? And if you can't carry out that great idea you had of love on the kitchen table because the three-year-old has a way of getting up in search of a drink of water, well, you can come up with another, equally delightful idea, can't you? And you can get a secure lock for the bedroom door.

As much as anything else, a couple who want to keep things alive for themselves have to have time away from children as well as telephones, neighbors, and Girl Scout cookie peddlers. For a long time, my man and I have had a great thing going for us. We have one day out of the week we call our "hand-holding" day. Our name for it, as you may have guessed, is an understatement of what goes on. It's a day which may include discovery of a little Armenian restaurant, strolling through bookstores, a ride on the ferry, a visit to the zoo, a picnic, roller derby game, X-rated movie, or evening at a jazz concert. And it may include a very special afternoon in a hotel room. Whatever happens, it's our day—all ours. Without those "hand-holding" days, our life would lack the spices that give it a delicious flavor.

Before you say it, I will: I know we're lucky. Not every couple can find time to have one whole day each week for themselves. But I feel reasonably sure, from what I hear from many unhappy gals, that more time can be set aside for the two of them than that one-evening-out-to-dinner-each-month routine of so many men.

I know it doesn't have to become an either-or choice when you have children: lovers or parents. You can spend more than enough time with your kids to do a first-rate job as parents without letting your romance atrophy. Nothing will make you hate kids faster than having them along every time you go somewhere. Talk about a breeding ground for frustration: I know couples married ten years or more who have never vacationed without their children. How's that for turning parenthood into a rack and thumbscrews? It has got to be either a guilt hang-up ("We would feel terrible leaving the children at home while we were away having fun") or they can't stand being alone together. If it's guilt, they should straighten out their thinking. What better way to hand a big bundle of guilt to kids than to have them grow up with parents who spend their time hanging on a cross for them. And if a couple can't take one another's company, well what can I say?

Maybe you only have a couple of weeks off each year, but that doesn't mean you have to spend it all with the kids. You can do something with them for a week and then the two of you take off and shack up the second week. And for the sake of sanity, don't blow your vacation visiting relatives. That's not a vacation. There are also opportunities through the year for mini-vacations. Even one day off a week can give you time for an overnight together once every month or so. Those overnights can build memories that will ride your romance through many a storm. For you it may be little more than a break from the routine and a day of uninhibited fun together, but ask your gal what it means to her. I'll bet it provides her with something to plan and dream for as well as memories enough to erase boredom. And it can go a long way toward keeping her alive and turned on to you for the weeks that follow.

I'll anticipate the two objections: money and baby-sitters. Admittedly, both can be very real problems. But both can usually be overcome—*if* the overnight is important enough to the two of you. If she wants it badly enough, she may be able to scratch some nickels and dimes from her grocery money each week to piggy-bank sufficient funds every six weeks or so. Or you may budget out some minor item or two (perhaps that golf game with the boys) and budget in the overnight. Besides, the overnight doesn't have to call for half a month's income. The object, after all, is to get away together. If you have the money for a suite in the best hotel or a weekend flight to Jamaica, fine, but even a sleeping bag for two in the woods can provide a more than memorable experience. Instead of a plush restaurant, a picnic basket. Instead of a cocktail lounge, a bottle of wine or a six-pack of beer. The important point is that you are away together. TOGETHER!

Baby-sitters are not usually all the big problem so many make it out to be. Unless you live in a retirement community (in which case you don't need baby-sitters), there are no doubt some level-headed high school and/or college-age kids around the neighborhood. If your overnight date is on a weekend, you should be able to hire one you can have confidence in, and without it costing a fortune. You can stay bound up in a "concerned parent" box with that "I could never leave my children with anyone else" (or "anyone other than my mother"), but that isn't concern, it's neurosis. Of course you don't leave them with a scatterbrained fourteen-year-old who is going to spend

the evening entertaining her boy friend. But there are
a number of sixteen- and seventeen-year-old girls who
are more competent at child care than their mothers.
The idea is to scout around until you find them. This
should be your gal's job since she has more access to
sources—other women with children. If she keeps her
list of baby-sitters up to date and you give her sufficient notice ahead of time, the two of you should be
able to take off whenever the time and finances permit.

A couple of further words about children and what
they may do to your love affair if you let them: Per-
missive parents have a way of digging the grave of
their romantic opportunities. Since they don't say no
to their children often enough or firmly enough, they
seldom have time, or even energy, for one another.
And the only time they can be together as a man and
a woman in love is after the kids are asleep (following
an exhausting battle of parent-child wills). By that
time, they're both ready to collapse. Never would they
send the kids out of the room so the two of them could
enjoy a quiet moment of conversation over cocktails.
That would be a "rejection" of the little tyrants. No,
instead they reject the great thing they might share together. We hear so much about the rights of children,
but what about the rights of adults? The fuzzy-headed
child experts yap about the child's need for privacy.
Well, I'm not going to say children don't deserve some
privacy, but I will serve notice on them: So do a man
and woman in love! They can get all the attention
they crave from that man of mine but they better
stand in line—and I'm first!

Back to that matter of the ivory tower: Maybe you
can't live in it. She knows that. But you can *long* for it,
and if she knows you want to be off in that secluded

love cottage with her as much as she wants to be there with you, it's the next best thing. At least when it comes to scoring points. And isn't scoring what it's all about?

CHAPTER ELEVEN

Why Not Get a Divorce, Take a Mistress, or Become a Monk

Marriage is a serious institution. So is an insane asylum. But there is obviously a big, big difference. In the former, the commitments are voluntary. And the inmates of the asylum often know why they're there.

I don't believe in kicking an institution when it's down, and marriage, contemporary style, is certainly a downer, but I think we ought to say it like it is when it comes to the matrimonial madness of the marry-and-settle-down set. Could anyone have come up with much of anything more depressing or more irrational than the connubial blah you meet if you knock on any door? Think of it. You have to pass a test on your qualifications to secure a license to drive an automobile, give haircuts, or sell real estate. But marriage and the Presidency of the United States don't call for many qualifications. You don't even have to prove you are mentally competent. Do you suppose there's a lesson somewhere in that?

There are many ways to kill a love affair, but if you want it to die a natural death, get married. Before you get the thank-you notes for the wedding gifts in the mail, you can have one foot in the grave. All you have to do is follow the advice and example of other "happily married" couples.

I can't tell you why men get married or what they expect when they do. That's something the members of your sex would have to answer. But I can tell you there are few gals who walk down the aisle expecting to wind up with what they get: routine, boredom, so-so sex, and a life that is as romantic as diet yogurt. Since he doesn't get anything better than she gets, why not forget the whole drab business? Chuck the marriage trap and stay alive!

You might, you know, go off to a monastery. It offers regular hours, no commuting, and no bitching bride. And just think: no arguments when you want to go to a football game. You just don't go. But maybe being a monk isn't your thing. You may feel a gal has something to offer which you would rather not do without. And outside of the marriage box, she does. She can do nice things for your ego, and equally nice things for both body and soul. And if you are old enough to have been shaving for a while and don't have a kinky thing for boys, I'll bet you find a bed alone a lousy lonely place, not even very good for sleeping.

If so, great! I'm all for men and women getting together to do what men and women were created to do in a beautiful way. And I think most other gals feel the same way. So why not have yourself a warm and willing mistress? Why not indeed? Any guy who likes gals and doesn't lust after a loving mistress has crippling inhibitions (or some other sad problem only a shrink could spell out). So let's admit it: a mistress has one hell of a lot to offer that a wife can't compete with. A mistress makes her man the center of her life. She makes a study of loving her man and becomes a professional in pleasuring him. When he walks through her door, she reeks—and I do mean she *reeks* a lusty anticipation of what he has to offer. And she has a way of putting it across which will always make her man know what she gets from him. You never hear of a mistress slopping around in a hem-out wash dress. A mistress doesn't sit across the cocktail table from her lover with dirty fingernails and stringy hair. She doesn't prattle endlessly about neighborhood gossip or the kids and their hourly battles. She is interested in her man's world, his ideas and interests, his likes and dislikes. She stays alive to him and to the world about her.

On the other hand, take a look at a wife. If she holds a job out of the home, the job often becomes more important to her than he is. At the end of the day, she still has her head at the office when she meets him. Or she greets him with, "I'm all wiped out; why don't you heat the TV dinners?" If she doesn't hold a job, she makes housework sound like digging a hole to China in a day with a teaspoon. She's habitually tired, seldom satisfied, rarely enthusiastic about anything he comes up with, and seldom the picture of a happy loving gal. If she has kids, they hold first place over her man although she bitches about them continually and blames him for forcing them on her. From the day of the wedding on, she digs herself into a rut. By the first anniversary, she is ready to join the other house fraus: she has become an insufferable bore.

So why not get yourself a mistress? It has been a time-honored custom in many European countries for centuries. In Latin countries, it has been more or less accepted, at least until recently. With something approaching sexual equality, middle- and upper-class married women everywhere have put their foot down and stopped being so tolerant of their spouses' kept women. But we know, don't we, that there are still more than a small number of married men who have little sex kittens stashed away in cozy love nests. And a whole lot more who have an occasional amorous acquaintance good for a business trip holiday or a late evening "at the office." There is one thing sure: there is no shortage of gals willing, even eager, to accommodate. Musical beds has become a more popular game than ping-pong even though we haven't yet sent a team to China. It has an obvious appeal to those of both sexes who are living out the silent scream of suburban, rural, or metropolitan marriage. So why not?

Well, there may be a couple of more reasons against it than for it. And I'm not going to preach morality and fidelity. That's for you to wrestle with. Let's just be practical. Money is one great big consideration. If you are already married and have reasons, whatever they may be, for not asking a judge to wind it up, keeping a mistress as well as a wife calls for a more than comfortable income—and you can't claim the mistress as an exemption. You see, one of the things about a mistress is that she isn't liable to be satisfied with being parked before the television every night. She expects a lover who will treat her like the gal he wants to have an affair with. And that means dinners

out, night clubs, concerts, sports events, romantic
cocktail spots, the whole bit that says a guy is turned
on by a gal and going after her. And if you don't think
that takes more than the cost of a six-pack, you
haven't been to a well-upholstered eating place recently.
Add something else to the budget. If you are really
going to go all the way in keeping a mistress (as op-
posed to just a once-in-a-while shackup), you're going
to have to figure in a tab for her keep—food, booze,
apartment, clothes, and tuition for her kid brother's
college education.

Even if you own three producing oil wells and half
interest in a South African diamond mine, you can
still get drained—and you probably will. But it will be
physical rather than financial. And emotional as well.
Keeping a mistress while still keeping a wife is simply
exhausting. Ask any guy who has tried it over any period of time. You have a wife you have to try to keep
off your back and unsuspecting. That takes more than
a little time and effort. At the same time, you can't
expect your mistress to sit quietly on the shelf to be
picked up and played with whenever you have the
time and the urge. A mistress is no different from a
wife in one major respect common to all females: she
can display a healthy jealousy.

There is also something very exhausting in deception which is kept up over a long period. Fear of de-
tection is so tiring we read about embezzlers who give
themselves up after years of dipping into the till simply because they are worn out.

And what happens when the game is up and your
wife finds out? And don't fool yourself. The odds are
heavy that she will. You may figure you can beat the
odds. You know, don't get caught with any motel re-
ceipts, think up really imaginative stories, remember

to be attentive to your wife so she won't suspect, get your trusted buddies at the office to cover for you when your wife phones, and take your mistress to only far out of town places where there is no chance of running into any of your friends and neighbors. Then you better hope for one more thing: a remarkably stupid wife. Women have a sixth, seventh, or eighth sense. I have a hunch this is another one of those advantages my sex has over you men. It tips them off to the presence of another female hidden behind the drapes or secluded in the secretarial pool. She may never catch her man in the act, but once she picks up the scent, that's proof enough for her. At that point, look out! The explosion could well blow up everything—and for good. If that's what he wants, fooling around with another gal is a pretty sure way of bringing it off. But if a guy really wants to cash in his chips on the marriage, why the deceptions? Why not break it up, move out, settle the property and pay-offs, and ride off into the sunset with the girl friend? The obvious answer is that he has too much to lose: children if he has any, money, status, and maybe a dozen other intangibles and tangibles.

So if filing for divorce isn't your answer, and keeping a mistress on the side comes with too much hassle and expense, and marriage is too much like a TV equipped coffin, why not go for the best of all, what I've been yapping about all through these pages: Tearing up that marriage license and turning the gal you married into your mistress.

Oh, I'm not saying you have literally to tear up that piece of paper (although I've never seen much point in hanging onto it—to prove or guarantee what?). I'm talking about tearing up that typically married syndrome—or sickness. This calls for a dramatic flip-flop

in both attitudes and actions. If you are at all suscepti-
ble to the influences of those living all around you
(and, it seems, crawling through the windows), and
we all are, then you have been well brainwashed,
molded, conditioned, and conned into what they have
bought where marriage is concerned. We all got it. It's
like being raised to believe the earth is flat. You don't
doubt it. Nobody you know denies it. And then along
comes some clown who says the queen of Spain has
fixed him up with three ships to sail off and prove it
isn't so. If you go along with it, you'll find a world out
there ready to say you're plum out of your tree.

Ask the question, "How many married couples do
you know who have what can be called a love affair?"
and the answer you most often get is, "I think most of
my friends have pretty good marriages; at least they
seem happy." Sure, but that isn't an answer to the
question. Somebody, I think it was Erich Fromm, the
psychoanalyst, said we have reached such a low point
in our expectancies of marriage that most couples
would rate their marriage as "good" if they simply can
keep from fighting. The suggestion that a man and a
woman have a good thing going for them if they live
with an armed truce is just plain *sick!* Yet this is close
to what most of the happily harassed married on your
block have settled for.

The individual who claims he has not been brainwashed into this marry-and-settle-down-rut type of
thinking has either never opened his eyes to what's
going on in his world or he isn't living in the same
world as the rest of us. We all were. And we continue
to get doses of the same every day. There is a saying,
"In the country of the blind, the one-eyed man is
king." I don't believe it. I think that in the country of
the blind, the one-eyed man would be considered a

nut of some kind. He would remark on a spectacular sunset and the others would write him off as crazy. If he persisted in letting the others know what he saw, they would no doubt get fed up with him and his arrogance. Well a husband and wife with a full-fledged love affair will find themselves in a similar spot. They will be as popular with their neighbors as a strip-tease dancer at a DAR convention. Lovers, if they are married to each other, have to be willing to be different. And they have to be willing to pay the price that goes with being different. The whole world may not hate you for having and keeping your love affair, but they will sure avoid you like you are a couple of certified loonies (which they will be convinced you are).

The husband who sets out to have a love affair with his spouse has to have guts enough to stand up to what the clods at the office will think and say—and it will probably be plenty. With the sexless sort of relationships they have with their pseudo-women, they have the idea that any man who claims to want to spend the evening with his wife rather than the office fraternity or a lonesome gal from the typing pool is pathetically browbeaten. If a guy wants to be a genuine lover, he has to be able to break out of the phony hypermasculinity bag in which all the little boys try hard to prove they're big boys (and never quite make it). He has to be able to see those clods for what they are. Take as a classic example, the would-be Hemingways who pack off to the boondocks with the boys for a couple of weeks to shoot up the countryside in hopes of hitting a deer (or reasonable facsimile thereof) or to squat, freezing their posteriors, in a duck blind. These are the sad Charlies who would never dream of taking a gal off to the woods with them. And why? You're entitled to your guess. I have three: They are scared to death of women, afraid every gal they meet is going to emasculate them. Or, they don't feel they have what it takes to score with a gal in the woods or anywhere. Or, they have a latent homosexual hang-up and are fighting hard to prove to the world they are not members of the limp-wrist set. As lovers, they just don't make it—period. As far as a gal is concerned, the only gun they can get is the one they used to shoot at ducks. But they are the sort of male characters who will give a *real* lover a rough time when he turns down their pitch to join in their games. They can't understand how a man can build and maintain a great thing with a gal. They couldn't; they're too afraid of getting that close. So they are convinced in their own little pea brains that the guy who goes home to a pair of welcome arms and warm lips is tied to a steel apron string. You can pity them if you want, but don't be sucked into their "honest, I do have hair on my chest" mentality. Not if gals are more important to you than ducks and dumbheads.

It is obviously just as important that your gal break away from the female counterparts of these males. Maybe even more important since women seem to become obsessed with attempting to influence their sisters. And believe me, she isn't apt to hear much of anything which is pro-love affair from the harpies on the block—unless the love affair is with the gas meter reader. She won't get much that is healthy from the women's magazines either. Nor from the TV soap operas. Of course, you can use your masculine muscle and *command* her to break off with the neighborhood witches, angry divorcées, and frigid feminists, but the chained-to-the-bed-post approach never works well to get a man what he really wants from a woman. On the other hand, any gal with healthy hormones can be se-

duced into doing just about anything her man wants
—and turn it into what she wants. If you measure up
to the challenge of being a lover and filling her life
with all sorts of great goodies she can get only from
and with her man, she won't be left with either the
time or interest for her unhappy sisters. And they
won't be able to stand her. She'll be too damned happy.

Begin by telling your woman you are through with
marriage. Let her know you want no more of that set-
tled-down married routine. Tell her you no longer
want to be a husband, and you don't want her to play
the little-wife role. And you sure as hell don't want to
live with a full-time parent. Tell her, straight out, that
from now on, you intend shacking up with a mistress
and that your first choice for a mistress is her. You
can then go on to spell out what *you* expect of a mistress. Note: I didn't say tell her what you expect of
her, but what you expect of a *mistress.* She can make
up her own mind about whether she wants to apply for
the position of your mistress. Give it some thought before you try describing the gal you want to come home
to. Keep in mind that what you should be talking
about is specifiable actions, not a lot of vague or ab-
stract generalizations like, "I want to be loved more."
Tell her how! It's the only way she can know for sure
what you want. And the only way you can tell whether
she's willing to swing along with you.

Before you go charging in to lay out what you want
from your mistress, however, you had better get your
role of lover straight. If you don't, she may chop you
down to the ankles and your new romance will be set
back to zero or worse. So quick like, before you start
reeling off all those goodies you want from your woman, tell her about the lover she's going to wake up to

each morning and climb between the sheets with each night. If you've played the married game for a few years, you may have a hard time convincing her you are serious. She may wonder if you have slipped your gears. And she could be resistant to the whole idea. Not that any normal woman wouldn't prefer a sensual shackup to the matrimonial morass. It's just that, well, Mother and others wouldn't do such things, and we were taught to listen to Mother. O.K., so she's skeptical. That should just make the challenge more exciting. (You do like challenges, don't you?) Prove it to her.

First of all, quit thinking of her as your wife. Think of her as the gal you have seduced away for a weekend. Try the following test: Go over, step by step, your last weekend together, starting with Friday evening. How did you meet her when you walked through the door? Like a gal who was waiting for you in an out-of-the-way motel? And then what did you do? Share cocktails side by side in a way that said, "It's been a long day, and I've missed you"? Did your words and actions express an intimacy while you dined together—even if children were at the table? And the rest of the evening? Did you romance her either at home or elsewhere or did you glue your eyes to the tube or otherwise accept her as just part of the furnishings? If you left her on her own to do the dishes while you were off doing your own thing somewhere else, just ask yourself if that is the way you take care of a mistress for the evening? And how much time did you spend talking with her? I don't mean all that garbage about the office and kids and the trivia that make up most domestic conversations. I mean conversation which excites, enhances, touches, and builds. And most of all, expresses love.

What about Saturday? Any better, lover? How did you spend the day? With your mistress? Did I hear you say she busied herself with all sorts of housework and/or errands? If so, what were you doing? Why didn't you seduce her into staying with you and pleasuring her, lover? Or were you busy with all those "It's the only time I have a chance to catch up on things" chores husbands and wives think up around the crab grass estate? Good excuse, what? Not in this gal's book! If my man wants to spend his leisure time with me (and I'm happy to say he does), I'll get the chores done during the week even if it includes laying brick. If the odd jobs have to be done, why not get them out of the way early in the day and why not have her by your side while you do them? But even if you had a few nasty little things you couldn't escape, how did you spend the rest of the day and evening? Did you have it planned? I mean planned for romance? In other words, if she had gone off with you for the first time expecting a great swinging turned-on time, and this weekend was it, do you think she would be likely to accept an invitation for an encore?

That's really the secret to success as a lover. Treat her like she is the most desirable and sought-after sex object in town and you are only one of the competition. Go after her like your love depends on it. It does!

Turning yourself from a sometimes amateur into a full-time professional lover, a real expert at the science and art of turning on a woman, often calls for a job of transformation. In other words, changing that masculine image and changing a lot of little things. And keeping the changes coming. Jot that down as *the* key to romance. At least *one* of *the* keys. I guess you could call it the art of *unpredictability*. If she can read you like a book, the book probably isn't very complex or interesting. A lot of gals say they can predict every move their man will make. They are living with guys who are creatures of habit, and the habits are so frozen they can be predicted like an instant replay on television. Think about it for a minute: Without the unexpected, the loving may still be there, but the romance quickly fades. And without the romance, a gal has a hard time staying turned on. Example: Let's say she has a strong taste for chocolate-covered cherries. So on her birthday, Valentine's, and Christmas you give her a five-pound box of chocolate-covered cherries. It's loving, but how romantic is it? I'm not saying you should switch to éclairs. If she keeps up her thing for chocolate-covered cherries, keep them coming. But don't make it something she can count on like junk mail. If she went away for the weekend with a guy she had just met, where would he take her? How would he make love to her in words and actions? What would he do to amuse her? To excite her? To give her marvelous memories? Of course you don't know. And she wouldn't know what to expect. It would all come as a surprise. And that element to surprise would play a big part in touching off those great fast-pulse feelings in her. I know I've made the point before, but it's a good one to make again and again. Keep her guessing. Just make sure she always guesses it will be something good which happens to her—that you make happen.

Women love surprises, big ones and little ones. But from what I hear from the gals I talked with, men shy away from supplying them. Maybe some guys think they look more masculine if they stay in a rut. A guy starts calling his gal "honey" or "sweetheart" on the second date and that's the only name he ever uses for her. After a year or two, how much romance power will it have? If you listen to the way some couples toss those pet names around, you know the words have become meaningless. For the sake of what you want from her, vary your routine and your line. Keep her off guard. Keep her wondering who the man will be who takes her to bed tonight.

Perhaps the biggest secret to keeping a mistress where you want her—panting for you—is memory building. No gal who has a thick mental scrapbook of memories of great nights and beautiful mornings is going to start daydreaming of another man. And she isn't going to turn into a fat frigid toad. The memory of one really great afternoon with her man can keep a gal turned on for weeks after and can give her some warm reveries to draw upon to lift her over the rough spots in future years. A skilled lover is an expert in building memories. He doesn't just *hope* things will turn out all right; he *schemes*. He knows her soft spots, and he works on them. He follows the basic rules of memory building: 1. Use your knowledge of her when you plan the memory event. Employ your psychology of your woman. Make it imaginative and romantic and something which tells her you had her in your lusty head when you thought of it. 2. Try to make the event *unique*. You probably can't always do something different with her, but you can make it something special and different when you set out to build a memory. Whenever you can, try to make the memory times as distinctive as possible. Remember, you want to make it stand out, a clear picture framed in her mind. 3. Avoid, at all costs, *tainting* the memory. Anything negative can taint a memory. An argument, a criticism, a gripe about anything, whether it be the service in the restaurant or the weather, an attitude which expresses boredom, a lack of attention to her, can all taint a memory. It's simple. Just approach that evening or weekend or two-week vacation as if it is the first time you've had a chance to be alone with her and whether you get a second chance depends on how well you score this time. With that kind of thought in the front of your head, together with a winning attitude as a lover, you will give her some absolutely fabulous memories. And one added suggestion: A lot of gals are collectors. I am. I'm not a hobbyist when it comes to collecting things, but I have a large collection of mementos from places which have high memory value with my man. He has given me match books, swizzle sticks, wine bottles, theater ticket stubs, and all sorts of wonderful little keepsakes which bring all those memories back into focus. And he picks them up for me. That's important. I could pick up the match book myself. I could ask the waiter for a copy of the menu. But when he does it and makes it a gift to me, it adds something special. It says to me that the evening or the weekend is a time he treasures as much as I do. And that's what loving is all about for a gal. At least this incurably romantic gal.

CHAPTER TWELVE

101 Ways to Pleasure
a Mistress

You have an active imagination. I'm sure of it. And all you need to do to keep her life purring is to put that imagination to work in pleasuring her. If you use what you've learned about her, you can't miss. In the following list, you may discover a few things you have tried in the past, a few others you may have thought of but never got around to, and just maybe two or three new ideas.

1. Bring her a single long-stemmed rose. (Not a dozen roses. One is more romantic.)
2. Write a love note with soap on her vanity mirror.
3. Send her a telegram saying, "I love you." Leave it unsigned.
4. Install a water bed.
5. Buy satin sheets for the water bed.
6. Serve her breakfast in bed. Include a bunch of wild flowers on the tray.

7. Have the menu from that romantic memory restaurant framed as a "no special occasion" gift.
8. Give her a shampoo. Make it a very sensual experience.
9. Turn back the bed covers on her side of the bed.
10. Give her a hand vibrator.
11. Add a copy of *The Sensuous Woman* to go with it.
12. Phone her on Tuesday. Ask her for a date for Saturday. Don't tell her where you're taking her. Bring a corsage.
13. Park with her at an inspiration point and do what you did with her before you married.
14. Give her the evening. Clean up the kitchen and do the dishes.
15. Draw a deep bath for her. Add bath oil. Float hibiscus blossoms on the water. (Clean the tub after.)
16. Install amber lights in the bedroom.
17. Get an unlisted phone number.
18. Give her a picnic basket for two.
19. Stock the basket with a bottle of chilled wine, salami, cheese, fresh fruit, and a book of erotic poems.
20. Take her on a picnic. Don't forget to bring a blanket and pillows.
21. Spend a day making a mental list of great memories you've shared and the evening talking about them with her—preferably before the fireplace.
22. Take her walking in the rain.
23. Phone her from work to tell her you were thinking nice thoughts of her. Don't ask what's in the mail.
24. Buy a set of poster paints and have an evening

of mutual body painting. Finish with a leisurely shower together.

25. Take her to an "X"-rated movie.

26. Make a date with her to meet you for lunch. Arrange to take the afternoon off. Take her to a motel.

27. Take her late night window shopping. End up in an all-night coffee shop, holding hands.

28. Write her a love letter, a long one. Send it special delivery.

29. Buy matching coffee cups, just for the two of you.

30. Invite her to watch a sunset with you.

31. Install a secure lock on your bedroom door.

32. Bring her a sack of hard candy.

33. Make a tape recording of all the reasons you have for loving her. Give it to her wrapped in sheer lingerie.

34. Pour champagne over her in the places which will tingle her most. Remove it with your lips and tongue.

35. Do the same with whipped cream.

36. Burn incense in the bedroom.

37. Send her out for the day. Have the house cleaned while she is gone.

38. Take her skinny-dipping. Be imaginative; you'll think of a place.

39. Give her a pair of sleeping bags—zipped together.

40. Give her a recording of a song which has memories for the two of you.

41. Buy her a pair of crotch-out, bikini panties.

42. Give her a foot massage and pedicure.

43. Go bicycling with her.

44. Buy a champagne ice bucket for the master bedroom.

45. Send her mother on a trip—a long one.
46. Send your mother along with her mother.
47. Buy a two-cup coffee pot for the bedroom.
48. Roast marshmallows for her in the fireplace.
49. Sharpen her kitchen knives.
50. Put a special effects stereo recording of ocean waves on tape. Play it while you have a nude luau on the living room floor.
51. Set aside two hours each night to share thoughts, ideas, dreams, and memories with her.
52. Take her away for a weekend on a houseboat.
53. Cover one wall and/or ceiling of the bedroom in mirror tiles.
54. Select a new spray cologne, one you feel expresses her. Spray her sheets with it (lightly).
55. Give her a gift certificate for a day at a beauty salon.
56. Install a telephone-type shower attachment in the master bath. Experiment with its advantages when you shower together.
57. Take her to a play or an opera.
58. Prepare a basket of fresh fruit and a thermos of coffee. Take her up to a hilltop to watch the sun rise.
59. Replace her lingerie. Anything which isn't sexy, turn into cleaning rags.
60. Take her to an amusement park—without children along.
61. Plan a surprise vacation. Make the reservations, arrange for a baby-sitter. Tell her to pack the suitcase, but don't tell her where you are going. Just be sure it is someplace romantic.
62. Resolve to spend time each day planning how you will spend the time you are with her.
63. Lay carpet in the master bathroom.

64. Take over the financial management.
65. Take a bath together by candlelight.
66. Clean the garage (basement, den).
67. Plan a surprise party for her with all the trimmings and decorations. Make it just for two.
68. Thank her the next morning after love-making. Tell her how great it was.
69. Keep your clothes picked up and on hangers.
70. Fill her cigarette lighter.
71. Give her an all-over massage with lotion and vibrator.
72. Repair something around the house which she has not requested.
73. Give her the front section of the newspaper first.
74. Start a charm bracelet of memory spots you've shared.
75. Make love to her by the light of the Christmas tree lights on Christmas Eve.
76. Have her jewelry cleaned.
77. Bring home a bunch of violets, to be discovered on her pillow.
78. Write an erotic short story for her.
79. Accompany her on the Christmas shopping.
80. Take her on a toboggan ride. If you don't have snow around, make it horseback riding. Or do both.
81. Keep the alarm clock on your side of the bed. Replace it with a clock radio tuned to tranquil music.
82. Float a pansy in the master bathroom stool. Wait for her to find it.
83. Let her discover you rereading the old love letters from her.
84. Tell (it's never too often) how much you enjoy being with her, how much you want to be alone

with her, how much you think great erotic thoughts of her.

85. Let her win at Chinese checkers.
86. Beat her at strip poker.
87. Have an oil portrait made from her photograph to hang in the office or the den.
88. Make love to her hands. Love them, kiss them, caress them.
89. Make love to her shoulders, breasts, thighs.
90. Start a collection of travel brochures for future memory planning.
91. Wash and vacuum her car.
92. Start a hobby together.
93. Buy her a collection of panty hose in various pastels and have her model them for you.
94. Install a stereo tape deck in the bedroom.
95. Date her at least once a week—without others along.
96. Take her to buy a braless bra.
97. Enroll in a foreign language course with her, the language of a country you dream of taking her to someday.
98. Take her to a football game. Buy her a large mum and a pennant.
99. Kiss her passionately (for at least a minute or more, not a peck) each night when you walk in the door and each morning when you leave.
100. Discover three ways each day to tell her you love her and you're happy to have such a loving, sexy mistress.
101. Put down this book. Now. Go find her. Thank her for being her, and for being your woman. Then find a few nice ways to pleasure her.

CHAPTER THIRTEEN

Testing Your Lovers Quotient (LQ)

A lover is measured by what he *does*, not by how he measures up to a stereotype. And not by his height, weight, age, or the curl in his hair, if any (curl or hair).

Want to test your *Lovers Quotient* (LQ)? Want to measure how well you are scoring in your efforts to pleasure her? O.K. First, go back to the list in the last chapter. Check the items to which you can say, "Sure, I've done that" within the last year. You are permitted to count it if you have done something similar even if not exactly the same, but be honest; bringing home a potted pant is not the same as giving her a single rose. Give yourself one point for each item checked.

Next, add to that score another twenty points. You get these twenty points for other romantic, loving acts you found to turn her on. Let's hope you earned them. If you didn't, shame on you. And watch out; there may be another guy hanging around the back door. Your total score is your LQ.

Now let me give my interpretation of the scores. . . .

90–121: You have just got to be the lover right out of a gal's finest dreams and erotic fantasies. Furthermore, that well-satisfied mistress of yours must be the most envied pussycat on the block. Whatever you do, for her sake, don't ever stop that loving. But then, I'm sure you won't. You are not about to give up your position as her lover; you've found how satisfying it can be.

60–89: You *should* have a pretty satisfied mistress, especially if you scored in the 70s or 80s. Just be sure you select ways to pleasure her with *her* in mind. And that's where communication comes in. Also, be sure what you do for her, to her, and with her tells her you *love* her, not just that you are trying to grab her for a roll in the hay or trying to play the good guy role. With a score between 60 and 90, you've reached the minor leagues. You can improve your batting average and provide her with a lot of additional goodies. But that's a fun idea, isn't it?

30–59: Your LQ puts you right around the average for lovers. Note, I didn't say the average for *husbands*. Where do husbands typically fall? Don't ask. The answer is too depressing! And for a lover, a score in this range indicates he isn't working too hard at the games of love. He may not be providing his mistress with reasons for packing her bags, but he isn't stacking her memory chest with luscious memories either. He is giving her an occasional fabulous night, a once in a while beautiful morning, and a once every six months memorable couple of days, but on an every-day and every-night basis, he leaves many gaps in the loving and pleasuring. If your score is in the 30s, you may not be providing much more than bed and boredom. Come on, lover, get with it!

0–29: Have you checked to see if that gal of yours is still around? Lately? If she is, consider yourself lucky. She is either willing to settle for very little, hung up on the bonds (chains) of marriage, or figures she can't make it on her own. And what about her lover? How much pleasuring is he getting? The men I know who manage to stay the youngest, most alive, happiest, and most virile are those who keep up their daily practice of loving. So face up to it, lover. If your score falls down in this turned-off range, you haven't been trying. Maybe you should take a long, honest, look at why. Maybe you feel you don't have to. You know, the old *once-you-get-that-wedding-ring-through-her-nose-you-can-forget-the-romance* attitude. Or maybe you're sure that gal of yours can't be heated up with a blowtorch. Well, maybe so. I'm not saying every female can be turned on like a light switch. But before you hang your explanations on that hook, be sure in your own mind that no other lover could have tried harder, longer, and with more romantic imagination. Or could it be that you are afraid of sex? Or women? Or romance? That great big he-man masculine image hang-up turns more guys into failures with women than anything I can think of. The hairy-chest guys can pat one another on the fanny when they play football, but they seem scared to death they won't look manly enough if they learn how to caress a gal in the shower. One further explanation: You haven't known just what to do to pleasure her. Most gals won't say, and a man can't read minds. I hope, for the sake of that gal of yours as well as your own good feelings, these pages have given you some fun-filled ideas. If so, start a program to put them into action.

And one last suggestion, lover: some evening real soon, when you have her feeling all mellow and receptive, have her read the suggestions in the last chapter and check those which turn her off or just don't give her good feelings. Scratch those checked and go upward and onward with those remaining. And if you tune in to her and her desires, you will probe for those romantic and erotic actions which will bring her to that peak of feminine fulfillment. And since it will bring you to the top of the mountain also, what could be greater?

Lots of luck, lover. Let me know how you make out.

ABOUT THE AUTHOR

LOIS BIRD, author of *How To Be A Happily Married Mistress*, is an expert in the field of marriage counseling. She is the wife of Dr. Joseph W. Bird, a clinical psychologist and psychotherapist, and collaborator with him on the best-selling *The Freedom Of Sexual Love, Love Is All* and *Marriage Is For Grownups*. The Birds, with their nine children, live in Saratoga, California.

We Deliver!
And So Do These Bestsellers.

Bantam
On Psychology

WHAT DO YOU SAY AFTER YOU SAY HELLO? by Dr. Eric Berne.
(Y7711—$1.95)

IN AND OUT THE GARBAGE PAIL by Frederick S. Perls, M.D., Ph.D.
(DM7299—$1.65)

GESTALT THERAPY VERBATIM by Frederick S. Perls, M.D., Ph.D.
(DM7292—$1.65)

BLACK RAGE by William Grier & Price Cobbs. Two Negro Psychiatrists examine the Negro mentality in this brilliant best seller.
(N3931—95¢)

BEYOND THE PLEASURE PRINCIPLE by Sigmund Freud.
(NM5381—95¢)

THE REVOLUTION OF HOPE by Erich Fromm analyzes the problems and hopes of mankind in a mechanized society.
(N4187—95¢)

PSYCHOANALYSIS AND RELIGION by Erich Fromm.
(NM5558—95¢)

THE FIFTY-MINUTE HOUR by Robert Lindner. The brilliant study of psychosis and violence.
(NM4388—95¢)